Introduction to Legal Nurse Consulting

Fourth Edition

Zoey Publishing, Tampa, Florida

Veronica Castellana, RN, BSN, ALNC, CLNI, CPSS, EMLS
Ryan Sanchez, BSME, Marketing Expert
Lynn Alexander, RN, ALNC, CLNI
Laura Buttlewerth, RN, ALNC, CLNI, CPSS
Wendy Duncan, RN, BSN, CCRC, ALNC, CLNI

Introduction to Legal Nurse Consulting

Veronica Castellana, Ryan Sanchez, Lynn Alexander,
Laura Buttelwerth, Wendy Duncan

Published by:

Zoey Publishing
112 S. Armenia Ave
Tampa, Florida 33609, U.S.A.
info@ZoeyPublishing.com
www.ZoeyPublishing.com

All rights reserved under law. No part of this book may be reproduced in any form or by any means, written or electronically, including photocopying, without the written permission from Veronica Castellana of RN MARKET LLC. Inclusion of brief quotations in a review is acceptable.

Edited typesetting by Veronica Castellana
Book design, typesetting & cover design by Ryan Sanchez

Fourth Edition Printing July 2010

Copyright 2006, 2007, 2009, 2010 by Veronica Castellana
of RN MARKET LLC, Tampa, Florida.
Made and Printed in the United States of America.

ISBN-13: 978-0-9760931-7-6
ISBN-10: 0-9760931-7-0

DEDICATION

This book is dedicated to the many nurses that have worked long shifts, hard hours, weekends, holidays, and nights. These nurses have worked many times without breaks, without food, and regardless of what was going on around them. They have stayed on their shifts when the conditions were unbearable. They worked extra hours because they cared about their patients and they were proud of what they were doing.

Now it is our turn to do something for ourselves and reap the benefits and rewards that Legal Nurse Consulting has to offer.

DISCLAIMER

This book was written to provide information to nurses who are interested in Advanced Legal Nurse Consulting. This book was written with the understanding that RN MARKET LLC, the publisher, and authors are not responsible or liable to any person or entity for any alleged or caused damages due to the contents contained in this book.

There may be typographical errors or omissions in this book. Content and information contained in this book are only current up to the date of creation of this book.

The mission of the authors upon writing this book was to provide continuing education to nurses. It was also written for those nurses who are or want to become Legal Nurse Consultants or who want to know more information about Advanced Legal Nurse Consulting. It is a general guideline and we hope that it provides useful information for nurses who are thinking about becoming Advanced Legal Nurse Consultants. This is only a beginning course and we suggest that nurses look to further their education if they want to become successful in the field of Legal Nurse Consulting. Your time and effort will be necessary to succeed as a Legal Nurse Consultant.

ABOUT THE AUTHORS

Veronica Castellana
RN, BSN, ALNC, CLNI, CPSS, EMLS

Veronica Castellana has a Bachelor of Science Degree in Nursing, and a Degree in Arts. She is a Registered Nurse and freelance writer. She had been involved with Emergency Care since 1995. She is certified as an Expert of Medical Legal Specialties, Advanced Legal Nurse Consultant, Certified Legal Nurse Investigator, Certified Product Safety Specialist and is the founder and director of the Legal Nurse Consulting Firm (LNC Firm).

Her Web site is: www.LNCFirm.com. She has consulted on cases for numerous attorneys in the Florida area and for the Attorney General's office as well as cases across the world in Asia and Canada.

She provides mentoring and advanced training for seasoned as well as beginning Legal Nurse Consultants, Legal Nurse Investigators, Product Safety Specialists & Forensic Analysts. She has created the only Certified Legal Nurse Investigator and Certified Product Safety Specialist programs as well as the highest education in the Medical-Legal industry,

Expert of Medical Legal Specialties. She hosts seminars, workshops, and conferences all over the United States, including programs such as Introduction to Legal Nurse Consulting, Legal Nurse Essentials, Market For Success, Report Writing and Case Analysis, Contracts and Fee Schedules, Success Internships for Legal Nurses, Case Strategies for the 21st Century, The Forensic Workshop, CPSS, CLNI and EMLS. She also has home study programs available on DVD, iPod or online.

She considers herself to be a Diabetes Nurse Expert and Educator. She is founder and director of Diabetic Zone. This is a Web site where she offers free diabetes education to others all around the globe.

www.diabeticzone.com

She has hosted online shows for diabetes at: www.diabetesstation.com

She has written many articles listed online as well as articles for different publications and magazines such as Vital Signs, Today's Nurse, Opportunities in Nursing, National Nurses in Business, and Nursing Spectrum, XPro News and medical legal journals across the United Kingdom. She has also authored over 31 books in Legal Nurse Marketing and the Legal Nurse industry.

She owns RN MARKET LLC, the first and only company that caters to full-service marketing and mentoring for Legal Nurse Consultants and nurses in business.

She previously was an instructor at Louisiana State University in New Orleans, Louisiana where she taught marketing, design and Web sites.

She has been a speaker for the National Nurses in Business Association, American Association of Legal Nurse Consultants, the American Diabetes Association, Medipro Seminars, the International Life Care Planning Conference and several other organizations and conferences. She is available for speaking engagements.

Ryan Sanchez
BSME, Marketing Expert

Ryan Sanchez graduated from the University of South Florida with a Bachelor of Science Degree in Mechanical Engineering. As a Mechanical Engineer, he has designed and custom built many items including a custom water ski for a teenager with cerebral palsy allowing him to ski with minimal effort and coordination.

Ryan came to RN MARKET in 2003 possessing many skills in graphic design and as a Webmaster. He has a tremendous amount of marketing, computer programming, writing and designing skills. He has written articles for RN MARKET NEWS that have been published and distributed throughout the United States and has created all banners, displays and advertisements for RN MARKET including content and graphics. He works at RN MARKET LLC side by side with Veronica as the Director of Marketing where he works to promote both RN MARKET and nurses in the Legal Nurse Consulting and Legal Nurse Investigating field. He has also authored several books.

He was an instructor at Louisiana State University in New Orleans, Louisiana where he taught Marketing, Graphic Design and Web sites. He has also been a speaker for the National Nurses in Business

Association, American Association of Legal Nurse Consultants, and several other organizations. He is available for speaking engagements.

Ryan is currently the Director of Marketing for RN MARKET. In that position, he oversees and manages the production of all marketing tools for RN MARKET's nurses, the marketing of all RN MARKET products and courses, and the development of all new products and courses.

Lynn Alexander
RN, ALNC, CLNI

Lynn went to Piedmont Technical College in Greenwood, South Carolina and graduated with her Associates Degree in Nursing in 1995. She has 11 years of nursing experience in a variety of nursing specialties. Her experience includes open heart and cardiovascular, telemetry, cath lab, labor & delivery, dialysis, acute care, cardiovascular intensive care, post cardiovascular intensive care, medical/surgical, renal, orthopedics, and neuro. She has been certified as an Advanced Legal Nurse Consultant and Certified Legal Nurse Investigator. Read Lynn's story in the preface section.

Laura Buttelwerth
RN, ALNC, CLNI, CPSS

Laura went to the University of Cincinnati and graduated with an Associate of Applied Science in Nursing in 1988. She has over 17 years of professional nursing experience in a variety of nursing specialties. Her experience includes advanced infusion therapy, intensive care unit, cardiovascular disease, post-op care, oncology, burn & wound care, geriatrics, and rehabilitation. She has been certified as an Advanced Legal Nurse Consultant, Certified Legal Nurse Investigator and Certified Product Safety Specialist. Read Laura's Success Story in Chapter 16.

Wendy Duncan
RN, BSN, CCRC, ALNC, CLNI

Wendy was raised in the village of Genoa, Ohio. She went on to Kent State University and graduated with her BSN in 1993. She worked in the Emergency Room at the local hospital before and after her graduation. When the Florida sun called her name, she relocated to be near her sister who also happens to be her best friend. Her nursing experience includes telemetry, cardiac care, emergency, outpatient cardiac care, clinical research, cardiac surgical and cardiac critical care. She has been certified as an Advanced Legal Nurse Consultant and Certified Legal Nurse Investigator. Read Wendy's Success Story in Chapter 16.

Legal Nurse Consulting 13

14......

TABLE OF CONTENTS

Dedication	I
Disclaimer	II
About the Authors	III
Preface	IV

Chapter 1:
History of Legal Nurse Consulting 23

Chapter 2:
Why are Legal Nurse Consultants needed? 25

Chapter 3:
What are Legal Nurse Consultants? 29

Chapter 4:
What do Legal Nurse Consultants do? 33

Chapter 5:
Who can Legal Nurse Consultants work for? 39

Chapter 6:
What types of cases can Legal Nurse Consultants expect? 43

Chapter 7:
Why become Legal Nurse Consultants? 45

Chapter 8:
Qualities of Legal Nurse Consultants 51

Chapter 9:
What training is required? 55

Chapter 10:
Roadblocks when practicing as Legal Nurse
Consultants					65

Chapter 11:
Legal & Ethical Aspects of Legal Nurse
Consulting					69

Chapter 12:
What makes Legal Nurse Consultants
successful?					79

Chapter 13:
What are the steps to starting your business?	91

Chapter 14:
Where do you begin?				97

Chapter 15:
What do you do next?				107

Chapter 16:
Stories of Success				131

Chapter 17:
Conclusion					173

Appendix A: Continuing Education, Test, and
Certificate Information				179
Appendix B: RN MARKET Accreditation
Information					181
Appendix C: Standards of Practice		187
Bibliography					193
References					194
Web Site References				195

PREFACE
By Lynn Alexander, RN, ALNC, CLNI

Just like many of you, I went into nursing with a passion to make a difference. My grandmother was a nurse in the mountains of western North Carolina. I grew up watching her go to work in her starched white uniform (which, of course, was a dress), her perfectly polished, white lace up "clinic" shoes, and her "halo" – her nurse's cap.

My daddy always said she had the reputation of "giving the best shot" around. She was a single parent most of the time and raised four children, two boys and two girls, on an LPN's salary during the 1940's and 50's.

"Pete," as she was lovingly called by the area doctors and nurses, was tough; she had to be. Times were hard and being a nurse was sometimes harder. I remember hearing tales of long hours, being the only nurse on a floor, and on several instances, having a Deputy from a nearby Sheriff's Department actually come and take her up the icy mountain road to work, where she would be the only nurse in the hospital. She would work wherever; OR, ER, L&D, Med/Surg... it didn't matter... she was a nurse, period, and a "damn good one". She loved what she did until the day she retired at the age of 75.

I had just started working in a small L&D unit when our family and her mountain community of "Happy Top," in Andrews, North Carolina celebrated her 90th birthday. She didn't have a clue where she was, or that she had probably either delivered or helped deliver half of the people in the room. But, when she asked me where I was working, and I told her L&D, she said something that I will never forget. It was in a language only a nurse, and especially an L&D nurse, would understand. As I knelt down by her wheelchair, she gave me some advice; probably the same advice that she had received 40 years earlier. She said, "Honey, you gotta watch those babies... they can go bad quick." I began at that point to realize that we do not choose to become nurses, but that nursing chooses us.

So, here I am, 12 years later, wondering what went wrong. I've done most of what I call the

"Adrenaline Circuit" – Open Heart, CVICU, CCU, ICU, ER/Trauma, and L&D. I give a great shot and am a "damn good nurse," just like "Pete". But, I'm tired, just as I am sure she was.

Like my sweet "Nana," I am the single parent of a beautiful, talented and smart teenager, Samantha. She'll be going to college in a couple of years. It seems as though it was just yesterday when I would take her to the Cath Lab with me after being called back in for emergencies.

How long ago was it when the first thing she would ask me over the phone, while my mom was taking her to kindergarten, and I was driving home from working 7pm shifts, was "how many babies did you help deliver last night, Mommy? Were any of them little girls?"

When I look back on those years, I often find myself wondering what happened. The passion for being a nurse, the same passion that had once been so strong that a 4-year-old little girl could share it with me, wasn't really there anymore. Or at least, I didn't feel as though it was. I felt as if I were turning into one of those old crotchety nurses with whom we have all worked and have all wished would retire during our lifetime. Was I becoming a (gasp!) "bad" nurse? Did my Nana ever feel this way? Surely not! What in the world would I do if I weren't a nurse, sell cosmetics at the Estee Lauder counter?

I started looking at my options. There I was, a 40-ish-year-old single parent with not much to show for the past 12 years except a bad back, a bad ankle, bad hearing, a continually worsening latex allergy, and a little nursing knowledge. Then, I found Veronica. Actually, I called another Legal Nurse Consulting course first, but soon realized I could not afford their prices.

I searched the Web and found Veronica of RN MARKET. After talking with her the first time, I suddenly began to feel that old spark again. I began to get excited about being a nurse once more, and I began the journey that has truly changed, and will continue to change, my life. My once forgotten oyster, my passion for making a difference, started to produce a pearl. Not only has becoming a Legal Nurse Consultant brought me back to life again, my friendship with, and my love and respect for the entire RN MARKET team has restored my faith in people as a whole. This group of incredibly talented, creative, and giving individuals has proven to me and everyone else that they have helped us "get our groove back" in the nursing field, that we are important, we do have something to offer, and that we can once again make a difference.

Thank you all for the love, kindness, and acceptance you each give so freely to all of us who come through your doors.

By the way, now my teenager calls me and says, "Hey, Mom, how many cases did you get today?"

Lynn Alexander, RN, ALNC, CLNI
South Carolina

22......

CHAPTER 1
History of Legal Nurse Consulting

Since the late 1960's, nurses have been utilized by attorneys to assist them with medical malpractice, personal injury, and other medically-related cases in dispute. Attorneys began to understand their limitations regarding the knowledge of the inner workings of the world of medical practice, and began to look to nurses to help them fill the gap. Attorneys also began to realize that a physician's review of a medical chart or case was costly and oftentimes not as detailed in their assessments as may be needed to substantiate a particular claim.

Nurses have general and specialized medical knowledge that can give attorneys insight into the overall aspect of a case. We, as nurses, have all reviewed and audited more patient charts than we care to remember; therefore, who better than a nurse to enable the attorney to see more of the "whole picture " in a medically-related case.

Hospitals have relied on nurses to be involved in various specialties such as Case Management, Utilization Review, and Risk Management. Nursing specialties outside of the hospital have progressed to nurses having advanced training and certifications in fields such as Life Care Planning, Legal Nurse Consulting, Forensic Nursing, Sexual Assault Examining, and Legal Nurse Investigating. More recent advancements in the industry include Product Safety Specialists, Forensic Criminal Evidence Analysts and Experts of Medical Legal Specialties. Insurance companies, managed care organizations, physicians, hospitals, and government agencies also rely heavily on nursing knowledge of the medical record to solve their problems.

CHAPTER 2
Why Are Legal Nurse Consultants Needed?

In a study released in 2000, by the National Academy of Sciences' Institute of Medicine's report "To Err is Human", estimated as many as 98,000 hospital patients in America are killed annually as a result of preventable medical mistakes.[1] These are only the ones that were properly reported.

A survey of a 1992 national pharmacy database found over 400,000 medication errors from a little over 1,000 hospitals and that a minimum of 90,000 patients annually were harmed by medication errors in the country as a whole.[2]

There are many more statistics and studies that have been reported involving injuries or deaths caused to patients through deliberate, reckless or negligent actions of people in the healthcare field. Medical and nursing malpractice has been the term generally used to denote mistakes made in the medical field which cause injuries or deaths to patients.[3]

As nurses, we have all seen those practitioners that offer and perform substandard care. The majority of these types of incidents are the result of this smaller population of people who need to be held accountable for their actions and/or their omissions. Nurses are the best judge of what should be contained in a medical record. We are experts within our own field and offer insight into the nursing process. If a nurse is to be held accountable for proper sterile technique or assessment of critical changes in a patient's condition, who best to ask but another nurse in that same field or level of care.

Advanced Legal Nurse Consultants can offer more hands-on assistance by way of writing reports in an organized manner to assist with depositions of medical experts or witnesses and to organize medical records. Assisting in live deposition or court situations enables the attorney-nurse team to catch discrepancies as they are being said, and allows the attorney to ask questions in direct response to the statements based on a medical professional's input. We can help visually demonstrate the details to a jury by charts, graphs, or demonstration of how a procedure should be performed. We are accustomed to teaching in a way that bridges the gap for non-medical people. How many hours of patient education have we all performed during our careers? This is what our patients expect of us, and most of us find great satisfaction in teaching and helping others. That is why we became nurses.

28......

CHAPTER 3
What Are Legal Nurse Consultants?

Roles:

- Testifying Expert
- Consulting Expert
- Fact Expert Witness

Areas of Practice:

- Medical & Nursing Malpractice
- Personal Injury
- Toxic Torts & Environment
- Negligence
- Workers' Compensation
- Product Liability
- Any case where health, illness, or injury is an issue

Advanced Legal Nurse Consultants:

- Offer services to organizations in need of medical records review, interpretation, or analysis.
- Offer services for plaintiff as well as defense clients.
- Can locate testifying experts.

Advanced Legal Nurse Consulting may be defined as a specialty involving the knowledge and experience of nursing applied to the comprehensive review of medical-legal issues. Nurses receive advanced education to provide a greater service to attorneys, insurance companies, government agencies, healthcare organizations, and other organizations. Nurses complement the direction of a case by providing knowledge from experience, education and research.

Advanced Legal Nurse Consultants review and analyze medical records, detect tampering in medical records, offer assistance with demonstrative evidence, evaluate medical information, and provide professional nursing opinions regarding the causation of injuries and the assessment of damages to individuals. We interview witnesses under the direction of our attorney clients to help elicit the truth in cases.

Advanced Legal Nurse Consultants also conduct medical research and educate our attorney clients about the results and other findings. We provide reports and other presentations to the attorney to help in determining how to further find the truth in the case at hand.

Nurses are more familiar with patient charting than physicians and can recognize errors or omissions in these charts. We can also recognize signs of tampering within the patients' charts and records to cover up mistakes. However, we need the tools and advanced training necessary to recognize what may be missing in the chart, replaced in the chart, or when a chart has been altered significantly. There are other tools and advanced strategies needed when working cases of this magnitude.

32......

CHAPTER 4
What Do Legal Nurse Consultants Do?

Advanced Legal Nurse Consultants can participate in a case from the beginning to the end. We can bridge the gap for non-medical parties, extract facts from medical records, and place them in an organized report. We can create graphics that demonstrate visually important points, help interview clients, locate experts, research important pertinent facts, identify Standards of Care, and more. However, these will likely be the most common and requested services.

When first entering this field, the chronology data extraction will be the most requested service. Often we find the paralegal with no medical background doing these for the attorney or the attorney doing these themselves. Once the paralegal has long standing experience, he or she will often do a good job for the average case. We are not usually called for the average cases. We are called to review the cases with unusual circumstances or perhaps the cases involving large volumes of records that need a more experienced person with a medical background to review. These types of records can monopolize office staff time.

Advanced Legal Nurse Consultants are a great resource of information when reading medical records. We read every page and question inconsistencies. Chronologies are based on reading every page and extracting the facts in an unbiased fashion. Once the sequence of facts are determined, a list is made of missing records, important timing of certain events, relationships between one fact and another, and questions or details that need to be clarified.

Once all of the information is collected, a summary letter with a brief description of the key points is prepared. This will incorporate the legal elements of duty, breach of duty, causation and damages or injuries. With that in mind, a reliable source of written Standards of Care is located to support the impression. Visual aides to support the summary may also be used. Examples of these are calendars, timelines, or graphics that depict an accurate representation of the elements that most impact the case.

Once having been in this field long enough to understand the process, new roles will emerge. The attorneys gain trust in our abilities and begin asking for our attendance at depositions, mediations, or court appearances. We may even participate in the client interviewing process to improve our overall understanding of the case and how the events unfolded. By asking a client questions, we may find relevant facts in a medical record or about the case that may have been missed otherwise.

Services:

- Assist with obtaining medical records.
- Identify, interpret, and review medical records for merit.
- Identify missing records.
- Screen medical records for tampering.
- Review hospital policies and procedures.
- Define adherence to applicable Standards of Care.
- Define deviations to applicable Standards of Care.
- Consult with health care providers.
- Develop brief or comprehensive written reports.

- Develop outlines, timelines, calendars, or chronologies of events.
- Conduct medical and nursing literature searches.
- Analyze and compare expert witness reports.
- Attend depositions, trials, review panels, arbitrations, and mediation hearings.
- Help interview plaintiff and defense clients, witnesses, and experts.
- Identify factors that caused or contributed to the alleged damages and injuries.
- Identify and locate expert witnesses.
- Assist in exhibit preparations.
- Prepare interrogatories.

Types of Reports:

- Verbal
- Narrative
- Outline
- Timeline
- Calendar
- Chronological

Reports can be created with comments or without comments.

Length of Reports:

- Brief – 1-15 pages.
  Preparation time is approximately 20-25 hours.
- Moderate – 16-50 pages.
  Preparation time is approximately 25-50 hours.
- Comprehensive – 50 pages or more.
  Preparation time is approximately 50 hours.

Service Schedule:

- Initial Phone Consultation
- Initial Case Screening
- Retainer Fee
- Review and Analysis of Medical Report
- Medical Research
- Written Report
- Demonstrative Evidence
- Case Presentation
- Phone Consultation
- Testifying Expert
- Fact Expert Witness
- Locating Testifying Expert
- Locating Consulting Expert

38……

CHAPTER 5
Who Can Legal Nurse Consultants Work For?

Advanced Legal Nurse Consultants are found in places such as health management organizations, hospitals, independent practice, insurance companies, law firms, and government agencies.

Legal Nurses in the hospital setting are usually working in or with the Risk Management department. They are the people telling us how to complete the required documentation on our patients. They are also telling us scary tales of the nurses who have made mistakes. We all hate those stories because usually one of them seems like just dumb luck, and it could just as easily have been one of us that it happened to. We all know that we need to fill out this paper for state requirements and this one for Joint Commission, etc. Often it seems as if all of the required documentation is for everyone except the patient.

Risk Management nurses often review incident reports involving procedures and analyze how to remedy a situation. Usually, either the practitioner needs more education on a particular subject or procedure, or the process itself needs to be improved in order to prevent the mistake from being made again. For example, all of us have heard of surgery being performed on the wrong extremity due to the improper or lack of marking the correct body part. This usually has more to do with a failure in the actual process. If the process for marking a surgical site is double or triple checking and marking the site in a manner which can be seen even when draped, it is unlikely that mistakes involving the wrong operative site will occur. If all nurses form the habit of asking about patients' allergies and checking allergy bracelets, it would be a rare instance that a patient is given a medication that they know they are allergic to. Risk Managers have the often thankless and frustrating task of trying to make hospitals a safer place for the patient, employee, and visitor.

Advanced Legal Nurse Consultants in the law firm and independent practice settings essentially do a lot of the same things. Advanced Legal Nurse

Consultants work directly for the attorney client to review cases and organize the medical information regarding these cases. We can also prepare courtroom demonstrative evidence, deposition questions, and interrogatories.

Working as independent Advanced Legal Nurse Consultants, we can choose whether or not to accept a case. After reviewing a record, we take a side. If it happens to not be the side of the attorney who hired us to review the case for merit, we will discuss with him or her our thoughts. At that point it will be decided whether or not we will proceed with the case from a data extraction perspective.

In-house Legal Nurse Consultants cannot be expert witnesses, whereas independent Legal Nurse Consultants can. It would be a conflict of interest. We cannot be unbiased in our opinion on the stand due to a possible fear of losing our job. It may not be a real fear, but the opposing attorney would certainly paint a lovely picture for the jurors. We may be able to assist in interviewing experts, but independent nurses more often network and can locate those experts.

Let's think outside the box. Where can a nurse review medical records? Anywhere. Random chart audits for quality might be something a smaller office, nursing home, or assisted living facility hasn't thought of yet. Remember that Advanced Legal Nurse Consultants are held to a standard. If we are reviewing a medical record for merit, we should be hired by an attorney. If we are reviewing a medical record for quality of care, this is a little different and may fall into more of a Risk Management role.

The idea is that nurses are needed everywhere. Try all of those places that come to mind, we might find a new niche. However, don't spend a great deal of time on something that isn't proven to produce income. The idea is to produce income, not to lose our shirts chasing things that do not produce.

CHAPTER 6
What Types of Cases Can Legal Nurse Consultants Expect?

Nurses can review any medical record. Medical records that need to be reviewed are primarily in cases of personal injury, medical and nursing malpractice, and workers' compensation.

We are often called upon for medical and nursing malpractice cases because we know how the hospitals, doctor's offices, and nursing homes generally function. This allows us to easily navigate through medical charts and find issues that many non-medical reviewers miss. We know what to expect when a patient is admitted with a diagnosis of chest pain, abdominal pain, or shortness of breath. There are universal standards that should be followed for these cases, and nurses can spot them when they are missing. The same goes for outpatient or long term care. There are general standards that all nurses should know.

Even if we have never worked in a nursing home, we still have medical knowledge to be able to pull facts from a situation and organize it to provide an attorney insight. We may find we need to ask a question or two from someone who has worked in a nursing home. Those same nurses may call us with questions about our specialty. Asking the questions that help us with the case makes us better Advanced Legal Nurse Consultants, not weaker ones.

In personal injury and workers' compensation cases, we may find that we review many years of medical history plus the treatments for the injury. Usually, we will be asked to review those cases that are clouded with past medical issues that make it difficult to know causal relationship. An example would be someone who has a history of neck or back problems. If that person was in an auto accident and had neck pain, how would we differentiate what was caused by the accident? We would list prior diagnostic findings and treatments and compare those to the post-injury list. Then, we would try to find a way to highlight the important differences with graphs, charts, or calendars.

CHAPTER 7
Why Become Legal Nurse Consultants?

Advanced Legal Nurse Consulting is a way to use our knowledge and expertise in a new environment. What's the appeal? Most Advanced Legal Nurse Consultants seek similar things for different reasons. The money is good, potentially great. The freedom experienced from taking control of when and where we work and the personal satisfaction that comes when we see the difference that we can make in a client's life are all part of the package.

As Advanced Legal Nurse Consultants, we can make on average $125-$500/per hour depending on which part of the country we live in and how many years we have been working in the field. This is great money. The reality is that we have to get the work and be able to bill for our time. Even though the money is good, we will not start billing 40 hours/week. It takes persistence, but we can see great rewards for hard work and diligence.

We may find a wide range of incomes by asking those who work in the field. If we are nurses on staff with attorneys, our salaries will be less but we will receive benefits. Our salaries would likely be similar to comparable autonomous nursing positions in our regions. Independent Legal Nurses will have larger ranges due to different variables. The obvious variables can be:

- How many hours do we want to work?
- How many hours can we work?
- How good at marketing are we?
- Do we follow through with client requests?
- When we are busy, will we subcontract?

Independent Advanced Legal Nurse Consultants can make great money if we are skilled, confident, and have a sense for business. We have heard some say they aspire to make $200,000 annually. It has been done. We have also spoken to several Certified Public Accountants who have stated that the Legal Nurse Consultants that they are hired by have produced six figure incomes. We also have nurses who have utilized our training to make over one to two million dollars.

Money helps, but it isn't everything. Independence is what most of us seek. We all look for this for various reasons. Our most compelling reasons are usually our children and families. Many of us are finding that we "want our cake and eat it too". Being a nurse allows us a vast number of working environment options, but nothing like those allowed by being Advanced Legal Nurse Consultants. We can work when we choose, around dance recitals and soccer games. It is hard work, but we can make the most of our time and get the job done.

Some might ask what we are doing with all of our "free time" or our spouses may suddenly start asking us to do more around the house. Please refer them to *"The Legal Nurse Marketing Handbook"*. If they read it and still don't get it, refer them to the list of people we called and the marketing materials that we printed, ordered, and/or mailed that day. What about the bookkeeping class we took, the attorneys that we met with, and the new software manuals we read and are trying to learn? To be successful, we must stay busy and put into our job what we want to produce in results. Independence is great, but it is not without hard work.

We cannot forget that we are nurses at heart. We chose this profession and eagerly embraced the rewards of job satisfaction. We saw the acute MI patient through CPR and defibrillation, and after recovery, watched as he walked out of the hospital holding hands with his wife. We pushed the IV thrombolytic for the 45-year-old woman who came into the ER dysphasic with right-sided paralysis. She later sent our department a note of thanks with a picture of her at her daughter's wedding.

The rewards for Advanced Legal Nurse Consultants are a little different. Our services are called upon usually because something went wrong. We may not be the ones to save the day but we can help discover the truth. This is where the problem or mystery solver in us plays a part. When we review a medical record, we are first looking for the step-by-step events as they happened. Until we understand the course of events, duty is not always clear. If a patient arrives with complaints of abdominal pain and dies, we want to know what happened to the patient every step of the way to know where or if his practitioners breached their duty to diagnose and treat him.

We can also help the victim of injury. If we have ever seen someone chronically affected by an automobile collision, we know that the victim will never be the same again. Nothing can change the suffering that the victim has endured. However, by helping the attorney, we can help the victim obtain some peace of mind by getting reimbursement for expenses and suffering from the accident, and even help improve quality of life. Satisfaction can be felt in finding the missing piece of the puzzle in a case that may have been difficult to win. This applies to defense, as well as, plaintiff cases.

50......

CHAPTER 8
Qualities of Legal Nurse Consultants

Advanced Legal Nurse Consultants practice in a variety of areas all across the country, but there are common threads among those who succeed. Some of the best qualities to have or promote personally and professionally are confidence, persistence, consistency, attention to the details, desire to find the answers, and the diligence to pull it all together.

The misconception among many nurses is that Advanced Legal Nurse Consultants need to know everything. The truth is that we need to be willing to work hard to find what is needed when reviewing and analyzing the medical records. It's impossible to know it all, but nurses have a lot of overall knowledge that leads us to locate the answers and tie all of the facts together.

Confidence is one of the more important qualities to have. It can be learned but takes time. Many nurses have low self-esteem after working in hospitals for so many years and not being appreciated. Some of the best self-help authors promote techniques for success. Simply accepting that we are only in control of our reactions to life, not the actions of others, can alone promote confidence. An example of this would be that we cannot be in control of whether or not an attorney calls us for a case, but we can control ourselves and our reactions. We can call the attorney on a regular basis, send information so he or she remembers our name, call the intake specialist and reinforce our desire to help. All of these things will turn the tides of control. Eventually, he or she will need someone to help and we will have laid the foundation.

Instead of focusing on the things we don't know, we need to pride ourselves in what we do know. If we have never worked in OB, dialysis, oncology, or orthopedics, don't think of it as something we don't know. Think about how fun it will be to explore these new frontiers and apply what we learn. Most of us think of ourselves as "average" nurses. Attorneys do not know that "average" nurses can help them as much as we can. However, the truth is that we know more than they do about what they need. That's a start. We have a faster ability to learn something new to us in the field of medicine than they do. We don't see terminology as an obstacle. They do. Our experience is valuable and we need to think, feel, and breathe that thought. Believe it and those attorneys will give us the chance to prove it.

54......

CHAPTER 9
What Training is Required?

As Legal Nurse Consultants began to form associations in order to promote the networking and training of nurses in the medical-legal field, this led to certificate and certification programs across the United States. These programs are in place to provide a form of standardized education and advanced training. However, not all programs are the same.

General Information about Certification Programs:

There are differences between obtaining a certificate and obtaining certification within a specialized program. When obtaining a certificate, a person is usually exposed to new information in an educational environment. The course content is determined by the specific institution and is not standardized. The certificate shows that the person attended the training and has knowledge of that specific course of instruction.

When obtaining certification, the person will have professional experience in the areas of instruction provided. An assessment of the person's skills, knowledge, and competency are required for the certification (usually through a comprehensive examination), and the assessment is usually completed by a third party organization who is involved in setting and maintaining standards for the particular industry or profession. The certification process has requirements concerning on-going education and training to be performed in order for the person to stay current in his or her profession. The certification usually provides the opportunity to use the certification credentials after the person's name.

- Nurses do not need a certificate or certification to practice as Legal Nurse Consultants.
- Nurses can practice as Legal Nurse Consultants in any state.
- Nurses do not need nursing licenses in any other states to practice as Legal Nurse Consultants in that state.

- Nurses need to have current nursing licenses to practice as Legal Nurse Consultants. We can then place Legal Nurse Consultant or LNC on our marketing items.
- There are no formal requirements to practice as Legal Nurse Consultants.
- Nurses may want to get formal training so that we can learn what is expected while working as Legal Nurse Consultants.

Formal training is not required but is recommended. Nurses benefit from a structured introduction to Legal Nurse Consulting course and a skilled hands-on course. Courses range across the country and may take anywhere from one day to as long as two years to complete.

Some courses are orientation courses or beginning courses and may only help to identify what we might want to do or may help us to recognize that we want to pursue careers as Legal Nurse Consultants.

We need to know the difference between courses that will introduce us to Legal Nurse Consulting and those that will teach us the skills that we need to possess in order to get cases and make money as Legal Nurse Consultants. We need courses that not only can give us an introduction into the field, but will also provide us with what attorneys want and expect. We will need to be educated, confident, and ready to embark into our new career with coaching along the way.

There are programs out there that do not explain this. These courses give us many examples of "what to do", but never give us the opportunity to practice or apply the techniques of report writing, or learn how to organize, tab and paginate a medical record, or even how to assist the attorneys in developing evidence which could be crucial to the cases. We need programs that will provide us with the knowledge we need and the means to utilize that knowledge to practice with success as Legal Nurse Consultants.

Some courses are certificate courses. A certificate states that we have taken a course. However, it does not prepare us for certification and it does not guarantee that we will get a case. Many of these certificate courses are really teaching us how to be a paralegal and are not truly teaching Legal Nurse Consulting. We will find most of these programs are being taught in colleges and universities across the country as well as by some private organizations and institutions.

Other courses are not being taught by full-time practicing Legal Nurse Consultants. If the teacher is only teaching and not practicing as a full-time Legal Nurse Consultant, where is his or her training coming from? Legal Nurse Consulting is an evolving field and should be taught by nurses who actually practice daily. At RN MARKET, each of our instructors do currently practice, have actual cases, and are there to support and assist you all the way through your career as a Legal Nurse Consultant. You get to talk directly to them at your convenience.

Still, other courses are being taught by attorneys or trial attorneys. If attorneys can do Legal Nurse Consultant work better than a nurse can, why would they need nurses to work on cases for them? Why do they call it Legal "Nurse" Consulting if they don't need a nurse to do the work? If it is a nursing specialty, only a nurse currently practicing in that specialty should teach it.

There are also some physicians teaching Legal Nurse Consultant courses to nurses. Again, this is a nursing specialty and should be taught by a current practicing Legal Nurse Consultant. After all, we wouldn't dare try to instruct them in their areas of expertise.

At present, nurses who take a beginning course still need to take another course if the goal is to receive a legal case to review, write a report, and succeed in getting a second case from the same attorney. Others, if they did not take a course with the right foundation to begin with, will still need to take additional coursework to have the motivational, marketing, and interviewing skills required to get the cases as well as real hands-on report writing skills to get a second case. You need a course that gives you the added confidence to succeed and the tools to carry it out.

Often, nurses are given false expectations initially and find that they could have succeeded by investing their time, energy, and money in another program that offered more hands-on experience from current practicing Legal Nurse Consultants.

The field of Legal Nurse Consulting is NOT saturated. This is a common misconception. Most nurses who go into this field do not receive the right tools to succeed and they just decide to give up entirely. These nurses go back to their mundane jobs and further pursue other certifications and courses when they need continuing education to keep their license as a nurse. How many certifications do you have? How many can you get in your field of nursing?

Most of the nurses that take a beginning course and receive a certificate or certification do not even practice past their first year. Why? They were missing necessary elements to succeed that they did not get from the course that they took.

Any course can improve upon your education level, but are you taking a Legal Nurse Consulting course for educational purposes alone, to make a career shift, or to supplement your income? If you want to change your current status, you must be serious about what you truly are getting in the course that you take. Do you think that you learn better with only 5-10 students in your class or do you think that having over 200 students at a time will give you the personal attention that you need to succeed?

Many people who have taken these beginning courses are desperate and they land on our doorstep as a last ditch effort while trying to get their first case. **They have taken other programs and have decided that they need the hands-on training that our course, LNC STAT, can give them. They feel they need the complete marketing and motivational skills as well as the report writing software and tools, and the guided interviewing techniques that RN**

MARKET also provides. Once this is completed, our students are walking away having had a great learning experience, are well on their way to getting and completing those first cases, and are receiving additional cases from the same attorneys.

We all need personal attention to succeed. We all need to have the right tools to succeed. We also need to have the skills, marketing knowledge, and drive to get us going and keep us on the right track to increase our business and keep us motivated.

When deciding which course is right for you, here are some questions that you may want to ask yourself:

- What is the fair market value of the course that you are planning to attend?
- What are you getting compared to the tuition dollars you are spending?
- What will it enable you to do when you have completed it?
- Is it really giving you the physical tools needed for you to use on your own?
- What are you going to have at the end of the program you have purchased that you can use to create your own business?
- Will you need to purchase other tools?
- Will you need to take other courses?

- Can you make the money back that you spent by getting just one case?

The field of Legal Nurse Consulting is changing rapidly. Keeping up with what is new in education will help you, the Legal Nurse, excel in your career. RN MARKET teaches the current standards of Advanced Legal Nurse Consulting that are used by nurses across the country. The curriculum book for LNC STAT is called "Legal Nurse Practice Standards."

RN MARKET offers continuing education and current information to help Advanced Legal Nurses know their basics when trying to start out on their own, or when trying to improve their current practice. The LNC STAT course helps to provide the links that most Legal Nurse Consultants starting out are missing. LNC STAT is a course that was created to tackle the frustrations and failures that Legal Nurse Consultants were facing in their practice. Many Advanced Legal Nurse Consultants across the country who have completed LNC STAT, and who are using the marketing tools provided by RN MARKET, are getting cases within a week after the completion of the course without having to face these failures and frustrations by tackling them before they happen. After reading this book, you will be ready to start the LNC STAT Course and get certified as an Advanced Legal Nurse Consultant.

CHAPTER 10
Roadblocks When Practicing as Legal Nurse Consultants

Why do many Legal Nurse Consultants fail at becoming successful Legal Nurse Consultants? RN MARKET has compiled over the past eight years the four most common roadblocks causing nurses to fail at getting their businesses off the ground as Legal Nurse Consultants.

We were making marketing packages for many nurses across the country that had taken many other courses to find that when they went on their interview, they were not getting a case. Some were getting a case but not getting repeat cases. Others were doing a case and not getting a second case from the same attorney. Some were not getting paid after turning the case in to the attorney.

These are the four most common roadblocks causing Legal Nurse Consultants to fail:

1) **Marketing Skills –**

  - They don't know how to market.
  - They don't know what kind of marketing materials to use that are effective.
  - They don't know how to make these marketing materials.
  - They don't know what works best.
  - They don't know how to get a case.

2) **Interviewing Skills –**

  - They don't know how to get an interview.
  - They don't know how to go on the interview.
  - They don't know how to get the attorney on the phone.
  - They don't know how to bypass the gatekeeper.

- They don't know how to answer the questions from the attorney to get the attorney to give them a case.

3) Report Writing & Case Analysis –

- They don't know how to do the report writing and case analysis.
- They don't know how to organize, tab, and paginate.
- They don't know how to do many different types of reports using their computer and other software.
- They don't know how to create demonstrative evidence with ease.
- They don't know how to WOW the attorney into giving them a second case even before they are finished with the first one.

4) Contracts & Fee Schedules –

- They don't know how to present their fees to the attorney.
- They don't know how to determine their fees.
- They don't know how to make an invoice.

- They don't know how to bill the attorney.
- They don't know how to set the amount with the attorney from the beginning so that the attorney is not surprised with the outcome.
- They don't know how to be paid on time or how to even collect on their case when the attorney does not want to pay.

CHAPTER 11
Legal & Ethical Aspects of Legal Nurse Consultants

When working on cases, the Advanced Legal Nurse Consultant role is one of a nurse. We are there to provide education and interpretation of medical records and medical issues. We are not allowed to practice law without a license. We should provide factual information and opinions regarding the medical records or medical issues in the case. We should not offer our expertise in areas that should be left to the attorneys and should stick to what we are experts in.

- Do not give legal advice.
- Work strictly for the attorney in the case.
- Do not work for the patient themselves. If a patient asks you for legal advice, you need

to direct that patient to the attorney on the case.

As Advanced Legal Nurse Consultants, we are held accountable for our work at all times. We should always give accurate information to the attorneys that retain us regarding cases regardless of whom the information may benefit.

Advanced Legal Nurse Consultants have a duty to conform to a specific standard of conduct at all times when working on cases with attorneys.

Duty:

Did the Advanced Legal Nurse Consultant (ALNC) have a duty to conform to a specific standard of conduct and was there a relationship between the plaintiff and the Legal Nurse Consultant during the time of the incident which has made the basis for the lawsuit?

A nurse must stick to the Legal Nurse Practice Standards when retained as an Advanced Legal Nurse Consultant (ALNC) for a case.

Breach of Duty:

Or, in other words, negligence is defined as a departure from the Legal Nurse Practice Standards for an Advanced Legal Nurse Consultant (ALNC). This would look at what a reasonable and prudent Advanced Legal Nurse Consultant (ALNC) in the same or similar skill set and level of expertise would do in the same or similar circumstance.

A nurse must act in good faith and follow the Legal Nurse Practice Standards when consulting on a case without causing damages to the attorney or to the client that the attorney is representing.

Damages:

The plaintiff would need to prove the damages that resulted from the Legal Nurse Consultant's negligence. They would most likely argue both the economical and non-economical damages as a result of the judgment or verdict against the client due to the Legal Nurse Consultant's negligence.

A nurse wants to make sure that they follow strict guidelines when consulting on cases.

Causation:

That there was a reasonable connection between the actions of the Advanced Legal Nurse Consultant and the alleged damages. The plaintiff would need to prove two items:

1) Causation in Fact –

- "But for" test - The plaintiff must prove that in all reasonable probability the damages would not have occurred "but for" the negligence of the Legal Nurse Consultant.
- "Substantial Factor" test – The plaintiff would need to prove that it was the Legal Nurse Consultant's negligence that played a substantial factor in the outcome of the case.

2) Foreseeability –

- The plaintiff would need to prove the Legal Nurse Consultant should have foreseen that their negligence could result in the alleged damages.

There are things that we are able to do and also things that we are not able to do as Advanced

Legal Nurse Consultants. The most important thing that we can do is perform all standard Advanced Legal Nurse Consulting functions found in the Legal Nurse Practice Standards. We should not practice outside of our realm.

Ethical:

Ethical is defined as being in accordance with the rules or standards for right conduct or practice especially the standards of a profession as defined by Random House Webster's Dictionary circa 1990 p. 459.

- ✓ The Legal Nurse Consultant provides services free of prejudice and conflicts of interest.

- ✓ The Legal Nurse Consultant reviews all current cases before accepting them, making decisions, rendering opinions, or providing recommendations.

- ✓ Personal prejudices and conflicts of interest must be recognized, as they may interfere with the Legal Nurse Consultant's objectivity and adversely affect the performance.

Conflicts of Interest:

Below are some things that should not be done as Legal Nurse Consultants:

- Do not consult on a case that you have already consulted on for the other side.

- Do not consult on a case against the hospital or entity which currently employs you.

- Do not consult on a case when you have information that is confidential regarding someone involved in the case.

- Do not change your opinions on cases or be coerced into changing your opinions. Be objective.

- Do not speak with anyone from the opposing side of the side that has hired you.

There are some things that should be done to avoid conflicts of interest:

- Keep records of all your cases to track any conflicts of interest.

- Never stay on a case when a true conflict of interest is identified.

- Let the attorney know you need to do a conflicts check before reviewing any confidential information or agreeing to consult on the case.

- Gather all the information you need to identify any conflicts of interest.

We should not work on a case where there may be a conflict of interest. If any conflict of interest is identified once we have accepted the case, we should notify the attorney immediately and remove ourselves from the case.

Confidentiality:

- Never speak to anyone about an open case other than the attorney you are working for.

- You cannot be paid for a case by contingency.

- Never accept gifts or money from the client your attorney is representing.

Fraud:

- Do not represent yourself as anything else other than a Legal Nurse Consultant.

Misrepresentation:

- As with fraud, do not represent yourself to others as any type of legal professional. You work in a medical aspect on the case.

- Never suggest an attorney that the client should use.

- Never work with a client who does not have an attorney.

- Never conduct an interview of the potential client on behalf of the plaintiff or defense attorney.

Attorney-Client Privilege:

The attorney-client privilege is there to protect confidential communications between the client and the attorney. Legal Nurse Consultants should not reveal information concerning an attorney's client or former client to anyone other than the attorney.

78……

CHAPTER 12
What Makes Successful Legal Nurse Consultants?

Legal Nurse Consultants do not become successful overnight. Time, money, and a plan are needed to start a successful business.

- ✓ Begin by getting your resources together to determine how much money you will need to start your business.

- ✓ Create a plan of action to get your business off the ground and to determine what skills you will need to make your business successful.

- ✓ Make time in your schedule and devote that time to your business without any interruptions.

- ✓ Do not let anything or anyone knock you down from reaching your goals.

- ✓ Fight for what you want.

- ✓ Accept rejection in style and continue with your plan.

- ✓ Market your business successfully.

- ✓ Deliver the message that you are trying to get across without running for cover.

- ✓ Do not procrastinate.

- ✓ Do not wait for everything to be "just right" to start your business.

- ✓ Get rid of the fear to start your business.

- ✓ Market even when your business is doing great.

How do Legal Nurse Consultants succeed?

Learn what to say to the right people, at the right time, for the right money, in the right way.

- Learn how to get through the door to begin with.

- Learn how to answer their questions and what to say to their comments.

- Learn the right questions to ask to get them to give you a case.

- Learn what to say and what to do to get more cases from the same attorney.

- Learn how to get them to refer you to other attorneys so that you can get more cases.

- Learn how to get paid for doing your cases.

Nine out of ten people will need training to get a case. One out of ten will get the case on his or her own but will not get a repeat case from the same client. That one will then need training.

The most important things to know are:

1. It doesn't matter how many potential clients you have, it only matters if you know what to say to them to get the case.

2. When you get the case…it now begins.

3. Failure happens during the good times. When you think that you don't need to market, that is when failure occurs. You realize it afterwards.

4. You have to ask for what you want more than three times, even from those that are going to give you a case; they put you off.

5. Selling Persuasion: Delivery – face, voice, body. 55% voice, 38% body language, 7% words you use.

6. Benefit – is what they want.

7. Fear of Loss – is what they get when you show them what they will lose without going with you.

8. Never tell them something you can show them.

9. Show them reasons why they should use you.

10. Don't cut your prices. You'd rather be turned down than suffer for taking the case for less later on. Don't give away your profit. Would they do their job for less?

11. Build value. We pay more for value.

12. What are they willing to spend on you on this case and how much money are they thinking they will get on this case?

13. Most nurses lose getting the case over the phone even before the interview. The rest lose the case during the interview. Some get the case at the interview and then fail to get a second case from that same attorney.

14. When you send information in the mail, hold back. Don't send them everything. Don't put everything in your marketing items.

15. You need to sell yourself before you sell your fees.

16. Marketing is too much work for most nurses to do correctly.

17. Many people use their current marketing items and fail because their current items may be like not having marketing items at all.

18. Working hard is not what gets you the case.

19. Present facts – ask questions, this is how you get a case.

20. Knowing what to say to the right people, at the right time, the right way, this is how you get the case.

21. Your "attitude" is why they are giving you the case.

22. Your cost becomes negligible if they think that they are getting value and benefit from what you are giving.

23. What would it take to get them to give you a case? Find out and do it.

24. Give them a solution and they will choose you.

Never Use Common Cop-Outs:

1. You don't believe that you could possibly fail with your marketing tools.

2. You want to try it by yourself first to save money.

3. You want to wait until after the...

4. You want to think about it some more before you start.

5. You do not want to pay for anything else to start your business. You've spent enough.

6. You have a friend or family member that is going to help you.

7. Someone else charges less so you want to go with them to help you get started.

8. You have made your own marketing tools and they are good enough.

9. You have a marketing or sales background and so you think that you can do it your way.

10. You have a certain way that you want to market.

11. You think you have done everything to try to get a case.

12. There are no cases in "your area".

13. The gatekeepers or secretaries will never let you through.

14. Attorneys only use doctors.

15. Attorneys have their own nurses.

16. Attorneys use their paralegals and don't need you.

17. You have nothing to offer the attorney.

18. You don't want to make a call to the attorney.

19. You can't be home to take a call from the attorney.

20. You don't believe in yourself enough to do the case.

21. You don't think that you can do the case or that you have anything to offer the attorney.

22. You think that we are trying to con you in believing that there are cases out there.

How much "Wait Time" are you using up? (Procrastination)

Wait Time
3 months to 5 years
(Procrastination time when you think about taking a course and which course to take)

Marketing Time
1 week to 1 year
When using someone and up to 5 years when doing it on their own

Adjusted Marketing Time
1 week to 3 months to 5 years
(You've decided what to do and now you are procrastinating again to do it)

Processing Time
1 week to 1 year
When using someone and up to 5 years when doing it on your own

Adjusted Processing Time
1 week to maybe never

Time Spent on Case
A few days to a few years per case

Some people will try to make perfect items or wait until the perfect time to start their business. Many say that they don't have the money or the time to start. No one has the time, no one has the money to start, but we still start and we still take chances. The ones that are taking chances are the ones that become successful. You can't make money if you don't start. You can't get a case if you don't have a business. Why are you really waiting? Fear to start.

"Turning points become learning points" according to Zig Ziglar.

So, how do you get cases and become successful? There are two ways to become successful; mistakes and mentors.

You have to ask yourself this...Why are there nurses out there making money doing this all over the country? If it weren't worth it, it would have been something we could not have made money doing and our fees would be lower.

For a more complete program in Advanced Legal Nurse Consulting, you should attend the LNC STAT course, which includes the Advanced Legal Nurse Consultant (ALNC) Certification test. This course also contains the MARKET FOR SUCCESS workshop which has been proven to enhance your chances of success. This program provides a hands-on and interactive way to learn what to do and how to become a successful Advanced Legal Nurse Consultant.

90......

CHAPTER 13
What Are the Steps to Starting Your Business?

Pre-Business Considerations:

Some of the things that you may need to do before you open your business:

- ✓ You will need to check to see if you have to obtain a state, business, or professional license from your state.

- ✓ You may need to file for a fictitious name registration.

- ✓ If you are selling products or services, you may need to obtain a Sales Tax Certificate and you may need to collect sales tax.

✓ If you have any employees that you hire either full or part-time, you need to file a "New Hire Reporting Form" for each employee.

✓ If you have employees, you will also need to file quarterly unemployment tax reports to the Department of Revenue.

✓ Check to see if you need an occupational license or zoning permit.

✓ You will need to open a business checking account under your business name in order to cash checks. Be sure to keep your business and personal records and accounts separate.

✓ You need to have a record keeping system to be able to balance your books.

✓ You will need to have a marketing and business plan with present and future projections.

✓ Check into the types of insurance that you may need. You may want to have liability insurance with errors and omissions included.

✓ You will need to research the name that you are choosing to use for your business name to make sure that it is not already in use.

✓ You will need to decide whether you are going to conduct business as a Sole Proprietorship, General Partnership, Limited Partnership, Corporation, or Limited Liability Company.

Starting Your Business:

Develop a marketing plan. Determine who your potential clients are and locate them. Put them into a database and research the backgrounds of their companies.

Find ways to reach your client:

- Send out marketing packages by direct mail marketing.

- Send press releases to publications or periodicals to which they subscribe.

- Write articles or letters to the editor that may get published and give you exposure.

- Join listservs, newsgroups, or forums that offer information to help you with your business.

- Frequent trade shows, conferences, or political events that your potential clients may be attending.

- Market your business through networking, referrals, and by your Web site.

Pick a name for your business that is easy to pronounce, spell, and remember. Check name availability and register your name. Get and upkeep needed licenses for your business. Decide on trademarks, copyrights, or patents. Register your business name by either forming a limited liability company (LLC), incorporating your business (INC.), or by filing a statement of partnership. Obtain an employer's identification number (EIN) if you have employees, are a partnership, or if you are incorporated. If you are going to be a partnership and have no employees, you can use your social security number for your business.

Design your logo to reflect your image. Do not use common symbols that everyone else in the industry uses; it will not distinguish you from others. If you don't want to pay for a custom design, create your materials giving them a fresh and professional appearance.

Make a business plan or proposal with start-up costs analyzed and written out using objectives and goals. Include a mission statement, a vision, and some core values which keep you focused on your goals and which let others know the direction you plan to take.

Your business plan should include direct costs, overhead, your salary, and your margin of profit. Start-up costs may consist of expenses associated with licenses, fees, certifications, education, computer, printer, fax, telephone, telephone lines, Internet hookup and monthly fees, office equipment, office supplies, marketing materials, organizational dues, insurance, professional fees, Web site dues and needed services.

Set up a schedule, and try to stick to it. Let others in your family know that you are "going to work".

Start your day the same way. Make time for family and friends. Take a break when needed. Get a lawyer, an accountant, someone that can fix your computer when it breaks or needs updates, and back up all your work religiously!!!

CHAPTER 14
Where Do You Begin?

Marketing:

The commercial processes involved in promoting, selling, and distributing a product or service.
Source: WordNet 2.0 @2003 Princeton University

You will need to advertise, sell your service, and brand your business appropriately to be successful. Marketing is what takes you there.

- It is your image – how others see your company.

- It is your company.

- It distinguishes you from others in your market.

- It determines whether or not someone will give you a case.

- It is how others will remember you.

- It is how you will make your money.

There are over one million attorneys in the United States. There is approximately one practicing Legal Nurse Consultant for every one hundred to one thousand practicing attorneys in the United States. You need only one or two attorneys as clients to have a steady income as an Advanced Legal Nurse Consultant.

Planning your successful business:

Time, money, and a plan are needed for any business to be successful. It's as easy as one, two, and three.

1) Time – you need to make a schedule. Use your time wisely.
2) Money – determine your budget and make a financial plan.
3) Plan – write out your goals with deadlines and rewards. Write short and long-term

goals. Write a marketing, business, and personal plan.

Execute Your Ideas:

- ✓ Get others to help you with what they do best.

- ✓ Focus your time on building your business.

- ✓ Pay affordable prices for quality work that meets your needs and gets you business.

- ✓ Achieve your objectives in planning your successful business.

- ✓ Do not procrastinate.

- ✓ Make things happen NOW!

- ✓ Get yourself together and get started!

What do you do first?

- Name your business. Make it simple. Not too long or too hard to pronounce, and not too hard to spell.

- You can have a title and a subtitle.

- Using your name as part of your business name can give you direct recognition.

Some other starter items:

- Telephone

- Fax

- Computer/Printer

- Address

- Web site

These items are needed so that you can print your materials for your promotional packages or for your business tools.

Business tools:

The first business tools needed are your stationery sets which should include business cards, letterhead, envelopes, and labels.

Marketing packets and introduction brochures are needed to introduce your business and build your clientele.

These items need to be made professionally.
Do not use an ink jet printer!

You will need to have a vision statement, mission statement, a logo or design with color, and a slogan for your business.

- A vision statement tells others what direction your business is going.

- A mission statement helps others to know what it is you are trying to accomplish with your business.

- A logo or design identifies your business.

- A slogan will add further detail to the main goal of your business. This individualizes your business and creates recognition among your clientele.

Marketing Plan:

- Determine your target market.

- Establish your niche.

- Market directly to your potential clients.

- Follow-up.

- Contact your clients on a regular basis.

The average consumer needs to see a name 27 times until they recall it in their time of need. You need to have them associate your name with what you do.

It doesn't matter what you know, it doesn't matter who you know, it only matters who knows you, and how they can contact you.

Monthly newsletters containing info your clients need will keep you in their minds and on their desks.

The Four Most Effective Forms of Marketing:

- ✓ Networking
- ✓ Direct Mail Marketing
- ✓ Web Site
- ✓ Referrals

Other Ways to Market Your Business:

- ✓ Press Releases
- ✓ Publications or Periodicals
- ✓ Exhibits
- ✓ Articles or letters to the editor
- ✓ Listservs
- ✓ Newsgroups
- ✓ Forums
- ✓ Trade Shows

- ✓ Conferences

- ✓ Political Events

Market to attorneys, insurance companies, other Legal Nurse Consultants, hospitals, government agencies, and managed care organizations.

Where can you work as a Legal Nurse Consultant?

- ✓ **In-house –**
  Working in a law firm, an insurance company, managed care organization, medical facility, or government agency that deals with medical records. You will probably be listed as an employee and will be able to receive benefits if you are working full-time for them.

- ✓ **Subcontract –**
  Working with other Legal Nurse Consultants or other types of nurses that have hired you to work their cases. You will probably make part of their fee on the case when you do the work for them.

- ✓ **Independent consultant –**
  Working for yourself with your own company. You will market to others to receive cases on an independent basis.

There should be nothing more important to do than that which you were meant to do. Market and make it happen!

A few words about success – No matter what, you will fail without positive thinking. If you always have positive thoughts, you will become more motivated to apply those thoughts to action to carry them through to success. A winning attitude is the most important motivator for success. Have confidence and believe in yourself!

106……

CHAPTER 15
What Do You Do Next?

RN MARKET offers highly effective Advanced Legal Nurse Consulting training, marketing tools to help you get cases, and other, more advanced training and certifications in the medical legal field. Most nurses start with our LNC STAT Certification Course which gives you all the hands-on and interactive training you need to start successfully getting cases and working independently as an Advanced Legal Nurse Consultant. They use the Ultimate Marketing Tool Kit to start getting cases and making money. Once this point is reached, many of our nurses like to continue their training with some of our more specialized training & certifications. You can also take advantage of our many resources, books and softwares at any time.

JOIN THE ASSOCIATION
INTERNATIONAL & AMERICAN ASSOCIATION OF THE LEGAL NURSE INDUSTRY (IAALNI)

The International & American Association of the Legal Nurse Industry (IAALNI) is the largest and only online community for nurses in any Legal Nurse or Medical Legal Industry. Locate and network with other Nurses with Legal Nurse specialties from around the world all at the click of a button.

If you are currently a nurse with experience in any of the following or related fields, you are eligible to join The International & American Association of the Legal Nurse Industry for the introductory fee of $100.00 for a one year membership:

- Legal Nurse Consultant
- Legal Nurse Investigator
- Product Safety Specialist
- Risk Management
- Utilization Review
- Case Management
- Life Care Planner
- Forensic Nurse
- Forensic Criminal Evidence Analyst
- Director of Nursing
- Nursing Home Manager
- Nurse practitioner

Once a year, usually before the Annual Indulge Conference, the association holds it annual summit. At the summit, the members get a chance to make a difference in the future of the association. They can network, vote for board members, discuss changes in the association, and share information about how they are doing as Legal Nurses, and learn from the experiences of others. The summit usually includes a networking party.

Association Benefits:

- Free Web Link on the IAALNI.COM Directory providing a list of Legal Nurses both in the United States and in countries around the world
- Free client referral service
- Discounts on marketing materials for the Legal Nurses
- Discounts on Custom Web Sites
- Access to the IAALNI newsletters
- Discounts on IAALNI conferences and training seminars
- Free Press Release templates to promote your business in the news media
- Free use of the IAALNI Logo and Quality Seal on all of your marketing materials and Web site

BOOKS:

There are some books that you can purchase if you are still deciding to become a Legal Nurse Consultant or if you want to read more about Legal Nurse Consulting. These books are great reference books that you will use throughout your career as a Legal Nurse Consultant.

1) ***The Legal Nurse Marketing Handbook By Veronica Castellana & Ryan Sanchez.*** A best-selling book published in 2009, fourth edition. This book has helped nurses across the country get cases. It takes a step-by-step approach and shows you how to market to attorneys, how to start a business and how to get the cases you want to achieve success

2) ***The Expert Witness Handbook By Dan Poynter.*** A second edition book used by nurses to learn the process and steps of what happens in a case that goes to court. It will also provide an in-depth look into expert witnesses with tips and techniques provided for those that are expert witnesses and those that work with expert witnesses.

LNC STAT COURSE

If you are ready to purchase a course, we suggest LNC STAT by RN MARKET.

There are five options for LNC STAT listed below:

1. LNC STAT HOME STUDY available on DVD, iPod, or online

2. LNC STAT 5- DAY SEMINAR

3. LNC STAT COMBINATION
   (combination between home study and seminar)

4. LNC STAT INDIVIDUAL WORKSHOPS
   (take one workshop at a time or just the workshops that you think you need to succeed with options of either home study or seminar)

5. LNC STAT PRIVATE INTERNSHIPS
   (Contact RN MARKET for options)

Now that you have completed the Introduction to Legal Nurse Consulting book, you can opt to take the test for continuing education and for a Legal Nurse Consultant certificate. Contact someone from RN MARKET LLC and they can tell you what your options are and how to sit for the Introduction to Legal Nurse Consultant test. You are ready for a more advanced hands-on course that will excite you and get you going in the right direction to succeed as an Advanced Legal Nurse Consultant.

Course Options: Take the full 5-day course, the home study, a combination, or choose an individual workshop.

LEGAL NURSE ESSENTIALS WORKSHOP
(1 day or home study)

The Legal Nurse Essentials workshop covers any basics you would need to be a Legal Nurse Consultant. This workshop is the foundation for any Legal Nurse practice.

Legal Nurse Essentials coaches new Legal Nurses on:

- History of Legal Nurse Consulting
- Legal & Ethical Aspects of the LNC
- Standards of Care & Deviations
- Hospital Policies and Procedures

- Medical-Legal Research
- Torts, Personal Injury, Product Liability & Medical Malpractice
- Medical Record Tampering
- Preparation for Discovery, Depositions & Interrogatories
- Selection, Preparation & Review of Testifying Expert Witnesses
- Trial Preparation & Trial
- And More

REPORT WRITING & CASE ANALYSIS WORKSHOP
(2 days or home study)

In the Report Writing & Case Analysis workshop, you get the unique opportunity to do a real case before you get a real case. In this workshop, you are walked through a real case from start to finish. When you finish this workshop, you will have no doubts about what to do when it is time to get a case on your own. This is a hands-on Internship and has been the best experience to get rid of the fear of the first case. This also helps in your marketing because you will speak more confidently when networking and at the interview. The workshop also comes with a Template CD software with 12 tools that you will need to write your reports.

The Report Writing & Case Analysis Workshop educates you on:

- How to use your computer for report writing using Microsoft Word, Excel, Outlook, Calendar & Templates for a timeline
- What software programs are available for Legal Nurses
- Medical record organization & review
- Fee schedules including types of reports, lengths of reports, fees
- How to review a case for merit
- How to organize, tab and paginate a case
- How to reference and index a case report
- How to create an outline
- How to create demonstrative evidence
- How to create a timeline
- How to create a chronology
- How to create an "Events Calendar" or "Treatment Calendar"
- How to provide medical records of interest
- Working with plaintiff & defense on cases

Bonus: Includes Case Kit

- Case Kit Includes:

- Book for organization of records
- Tabs
- A Case in Envelope to work on during course
- CD with Templates
- Handouts

CONTRACTS & FEE SCHEDULES WORKSHOP
(1 day or home study)

The material covered in the Contracts & Fee Schedules workshop is just what the workshop title implies, Contracts & Fee Schedules. This may not seem important at a first glance. However, this workshop is extremely important because it shows you everything you need to know about getting paid for your work. There is nothing worse than not getting paid for your work. This workshop also covers contract basics in case a contract is ever put in front of you. The workshop also comes with a Template CD software, 2010 edition, with 26 tools you will need to get the case you want and to protect yourself.

The LNC STAT course comes with VIP treatment, Champagne or wine, Chocolate, FREE RN MARKET Forum access, FREE MENTORING, (usually you can reach us 7 days a week 24 hours a day excluding when we are unable to answer the phone). You also have access to other Advanced Legal Nurse Consultants to help you with your cases or any roadblocks that you may encounter. Your certification exam is included. You also have access to the number one marketing package in the country developed for Legal Nurse Consultants, the Ultimate Marketing Tool Kit by RN MARKET.

The Contracts & Fee Schedules Workshop Includes:

- Overview of various points of the law
- Explanation of the purpose of each provision
- How each provision relates to points of law
- Letters of Introduction
- Email campaign notification letter
- Follow-up letter
- Professional Service Agreement
- Sample Contract
- Statement of General Terms & Conditions
- Fee Structure
- Fee Schedule
- Reimbursable Expense Report
- Letter to firm who uses MDs
- Letter to firm who uses RNs
- Letter to firm who uses LNCs
- Subcontractor Agreement

- Letter to Attorney using Subcontractors
- Invoicing
- Collecting Bad Debts
- Service Agreement
- Tracking Form
- Follow-up to phone inquiry of services letter
- Phone Consultation Form
- How to get attorney names/List of attorneys in your area
- How to get attorney information
- How to use information to get cases
- Contracts CD

MARKET FOR SUCCESS WORKSHOP
(1-2 day or home study)

As much as most people want to deny it, marketing is pretty much the most important thing when building a successful Legal Nurse Consulting business. You could be the best Legal Nurse Consultant in the world, but if no one knows about you, you still won't get any cases. RN MARKET has been doing this type of marketing since its inception. Over the years, we have become the most well known nurse marketing company in the field with marketing products and strategies that are more effective than any other. This workshop tells you all our secrets. Follow our instructions and the cases will come.

The Market For Success Workshop Objectives:

- Get you motivated and ready for success
- Teach you how to Market for Success
- Teach you how to successfully utilize marketing materials and Web sites
- Teach you how to promote results and increase your clientele by showing you how to market effectively
- Teach you modernized methods of marketing
- Teach you time management techniques
- Teach you interview techniques, role playing
- Teach you how to create your business and marketing plan
- Teach you how to set goals
- Includes Market for Success Workbook

THE ULTIMATE MARKETING TOOL KIT
The number one selling marketing package throughout the world for Legal Nurses in Business, available only through RN MARKET LLC.

Get a response with every 1 out of 15 marketing packets from RN MARKET LLC. Compare that to a brochure and letter of introduction that have an average response of 1 out of 100. These statistics are an average response for those using the Ultimate Marketing Tool Kit to market their business, and those that have purchased and utilized *The Legal Nurse Marketing Handbook* and/or *The RN MARKET Instruction Manual* that comes with the Ultimate Marketing Tool Kit for FREE.

Get the RN MARKET Advantage:

- Have a Professional, Custom-Made and Original Image of Your Company
- Use Researched and Proven Marketing Strategies
- Use Modernized Marketing Tools
- Get All You Need in One Package
- Add on a Web Site
- Market Your Company Using an Effective, Step-By-Step Process
- Get FREE Mentoring for Any of Your Marketing Questions

Marketing is what gets you the cases. Use the marketing tools that are proven to make you successful.

Ultimate Marketing Tool Kit:

The Marketing Tool Kit is designed to get you results. The Ultimate Marketing Tool Kit includes Custom Graphic Design, Custom Written Text, Quality Printing (if added on), Custom Designed Web Sites (if added on), a custom CD with all files ready-to-print, and Proven Marketing Strategies. You get all of this in one package for less than just printing at your local printer.

Everything you need to get results in one package including step-by-step marketing help. Includes mail-out sets, interview sets, business cards, letterhead, and custom CD which includes files ready-to-print. Add quality printing and a Web site to get all the tools you need.

RN MARKET conducted a research study to find what creates the best results when marketing your business to attorneys, businesses, and individuals. RN MARKET creates your marketing products using data from a research study. RN MARKET will create a custom design to put on your letterhead, business cards, and labels. You get up to 3 custom designs to choose from, and up to 3 modifications to your chosen design utilizing up to two hours of graphic design time. The written text for your Intro, Services, CV, Fee Schedule and

Sample Chronology are customized using researched and proven methods and formats. On average, clients who used this package and followed our recommendations have received 1 response out of 15 direct mail packets sent out. After your design and written text are complete, printing and your custom Web site are created if you purchased it. Once you receive your package, you will get FREE mentoring and step-by-step help implementing your products effectively.

ULTIMATE MARKETING TOOL KIT DETAILS

Services Included:
- Custom Graphic Design
- Custom Written Text
- Quality Full Color Printing (if added)
- Custom Web Site Design (if added)
- Step-By-Step Marketing Help
- Mentoring until your first case

Products Included:
- Intro Page
- Services Page
- CV
- Fee Schedule
- Sample Work Product

- Business Cards
- Letterhead
- Labels (4" x 3.33")
- Large Envelopes (9" x 12")
- Custom CD

Products Available as Add-Ons:
- Quality Printing on fine Linen paper
- Premium Web Site Package (Good for 1 year, no monthly fees, renew yearly)

Individual Product Details:

Intro Page:
Contains information about you, your company, and how you can help your client. The format and content is created according to our market research study and is placed on your custom designed letterhead. This page is sent in your direct mail campaign.

Services Page:
Describes all the services your company can provide for your client. It can also include a guarantee if you wish. This is placed on your custom designed letterhead. This page is sent in your direct mail campaign.

CV:
Same as a Resumé. This is used at the interview.

Fee Schedule:
A list of your company services and its fees. This is used at the interview. Also includes lengths and types of reports.

Sample Work Product:
A two page sample of the type of work you can do for your client. Your sample chronology is an example of how you or your company can present and analyze a case. You can choose one of our prewritten sample work products that we distribute per state or you can supply your own sample work product.

Custom CD:
A CD with a PDF and design files of each printed product included in your package.

Premium Web Site Package:
A custom designed, five-page Web site. No Web builders or templates are used and your site design will match the design of your printed materials. Registration and hosting for a year, email forwarding, search engine optimizations, Web

statistics and a contact form are included. There are no monthly fees. You may renew yearly.

Printing Packages:
Several packages of different quantities are available for printing. All printing packages come with free large envelopes for direct mail marketing. The printing we offer is high quality, smudge free and is available on a variety of linen paper colors.

CERTIFIED LEGAL NURSE INVESTIGATOR COURSE (CLNI) CERTIFICATION

As a Certified Legal Nurse Investigator (CLNI), you may work not just on one case, but on many for facilities in need of help with compliance to help them cut back on lawsuits. You may also work with attorneys or the government to help uncover fraud or abuse in hospitals or care organizations.

Many times hospitals cover-up the errors in a medical record. Either a hospital doctor, nurse, or other employee who was working on a patient may cover-up or hide documents, medication errors, or they may replace medical records to avoid taking responsibility for mistakes.

There is a growing worldwide necessity for Certified Legal Nurse Investigators due to the increasing number of suspicious deaths, trauma and other forms of abuse, to include errors made in hospitals and nursing homes. Many times, nurses are the ones who spend more time than physicians evaluating patients for signs of abuse through either intentional acts or unintentional error (medical malpractice).

CERTIFIED PRODUCT SAFETY SPECIALIST (CPSS) CERTIFICATION

As a Certified Product Safety Specialist (CPSS), you may work not just on one case, but on many cases regarding products or product safety including mass tort cases and class action lawsuits.

Learn how to minimize the risks in the product safety industry by identifying, screening, reviewing and reducing potential product safety problems.

THE FORENSIC WORKSHOP
FORENSIC CRIMINAL EVIDENCE ANALYST (FCEA) CERTIFICATION

As a Certified Forensic Criminal Evidence Analyst (FCEA), you will learn forensic theory and how to review, investigate and analyze forensic evidence and information.

SUCCESS INTERNSHIP

In the Success Internship, you will review eight case scenarios and build your confidence by practicing more skills necessary to get cases like interviewing and phone call techniques.

CASE STRATEGIES FOR THE 21ST CENTURY

In Case Strategies for the 21st Century, you will get additional training in useful areas like writing affidavits, medical and legal research, advanced interviewing, information security, finding expert witnesses and much more. Includes a custom list of attorneys and attorney conferences in your area for you to market to.

ANNUAL INDULGE CONFERENCE

Take part in the luxurious Annual Indulge Conference by RN MARKET LLC where "It's all about you!" Get ready to get treated like a VIP while learning from captivating speakers and networking with other professionals. By attending the conference, you will add another year to your ALNC, CLNI, CPSS or FCEA certifications.

You will receive Medical/Legal continuing education contact hours if you are a Registered Nurse, Licensed Practical Nurse, or Advanced Registered Nurse Practitioner. Everyone is invited. Whether you are a Registered Nurse, Legal Nurse Consultant, Legal Nurse Investigator, Product Safety Specialist, Forensic Criminal Evidence Analyst, Life Care Planner, Case Manager, Licensed Practical Nurse, Forensic Nurse, Advanced Registered Nurse Practitioner, or Health Care Professional, enjoy these few days with us in luxury, style, and comfort. You won't want to be anywhere else.

Luxury Conference Usually Includes:

- Continuing Education
- VIP Treatment

- Free Breakfast
- Free Luncheon
- A VIP Champagne & Chocolate, Wine & Cheese Reception (Everyone's a VIP!)
- Textbook
- Networking
- Speakers
- Prizes

You can attend the conference any time you wish or whenever it is offered. Every time you attend the conference, you get a year added to your ALNC, CLNI, CPSS or FCEA certification. If you are planning on becoming an ALNC, CLNI, CPSS or FCEA you can still attend the conference and have it applied to your certification when complete. These are also available in Home Study Seminars.

EXPERT OF MEDICAL LEGAL SPECIALTIES (EMLS) CERTIFICATION

Complete the Expert Curriculum to earn your Expert of Medical Legal Specialties (EMLS) Certification. Be among the elite Nurses who have achieved the EMLS certification and have reached the peak of training available in the entire medical legal field. The level of medical legal training achieved by an Expert of Medical Legal Specialties is matched by no other certification or organization. To bear the EMLS credential, Nurses must achieve the ALNC, CPSS and CLNI certifications and complete all CE hours included with the Expert Curriculum. The Expert Curriculum offers all the benfits found in our two smaller packages. Including the Case Guarantee, Active mentoring until you get your first case and Unlimited Call-In Mentoring. In addition, with the Expert Curriculum, you get LIFETIME certification, the most CE and training hours of any course in the medical legal field, two additional years of IAALNI Membership, registration for our once-a-year Indulge Conference, an upgraded print package for your Ultimate Marketing Tool Kit and our exclusive Business Invitations. This package gives you every course and marketing tool offered by RN MARKET LLC. With the additional specialized training included, you will have the flexibility to work a wider variety of cases and diversify your Legal Nurse Practice. Reach the summit of Legal Nurse achievement and success with the Expert Curriculum. See our brochure and DVD for more information and packages.

130......

CHAPTER 16
Stories of Success

I Got 45 Cases in Less Than 12 Months!

My sister found an article about Legal Nurse Consulting and thought I should look into it. I did little research and jumped into the expensive beginning course full force. After going to the seminar I had a graphic artist design my marketing material, using the logo I requested. I had spent nearly $12,000 so far. I began calling attorneys and trying all I knew to get cases.

Eight months into my new career as a Legal Nurse Consultant I realized that what I was doing was not working. My logo was very similar to numerous other Legal Nurse Consulting companies. Discouraged and ready to quit I realized that my weakness was marketing, selling myself, I have never had to do that. When I wanted a job it was basically a phone call away. I had the credentials needed to get the job in which I was applying. Now I was faced with proving to non-medical people that I was an asset to their company. So, I knew what I had to do – market.

Then, came the day that changed everything. While surfing the net I put in Legal Nurse marketing. The sun was definitely shining on me. Up came RN MARKET and wow, could it be - a company for nurses like me? Just when I thought it couldn't get better, I called RN MARKET. The friendly voice answered, "RN MARKET, this is Veronica can I help you?" Within a few minutes Veronica confirmed my fears. My marketing material and techniques were way off. Veronica had heard this saga many times before. The next step was to get the proper marketing materials and to approach the attorneys differently.

The amount of time Veronica spent with me, a total stranger, along with all of her advice, let me know my life as a Legal Nurse Consultant was about to get very interesting. They transferred me to the designer. After a few questions from her about logo ideas for her to design, within two days an email came. Wow, she nailed it, just what I wanted. Ryan and Alan were working on my Web site and marketing packet.

Ten days later, I received my marketing packets. The quality makes me so proud to have my name on it. Looking back now I can't believe all of the mistakes I made and would still be making to this day. That is if my frustration would not have put my new career on the back burner.

With new fabulous marketing materials in hand, the mailings began. Veronica called me a week later to check on how I was doing. Then, her famous mentoring kicked in. "Pre-call?" I sheepishly said. Veronica had me pretend she was the gatekeeper and I had to get through. Several scenarios later I finally had the courage to do it right. Every step of the way they were there for me. I got my first case that month.

Veronica is my cheerleader. I gave her a brief description of my case. Like an Uzi she started shooting out things I needed to do. A calendar time line---sure makes sense. Then, she told me about the computer software she has that would provide a great work product. Within about 2 hours she was able to get it set up for me. This is definitely the person I want in my corner. The attorney was very impressed.

I attended the LNC STAT program a few months later and became an Advanced Legal Nurse Consultant (ALNC). I also attended the yearly Indulge Conference and haven't missed one ever since! Now it was all making sense. Top quality, informative, real life experiences, cases to work on, time saving steps, marketing, contracts and much more. We were all so pampered, from sunrise to sunset. The confidence I have because of RN MARKET and their support is amazing. I went to a PRN status with my day job to allow more day hours to promote my business.

So, the cases were coming in at a nice pace----but, I wanted more! I made a call on a Monday afternoon to a health care law CLE program. Seventy attorneys were registered. I asked about an exhibit opportunity. Much to my surprise they said yes, on Thursday. Frantically, I called RN MARKET. The staff worked very hard over the next 48 hours to get me a PowerPoint presentation and tabletop displays. Just before 10 PM I received the proofs for the table top displays. The next day Ryan sent it to a local sign company near Cincinnati. Late Tuesday, I received the PowerPoint presentation. I picked up the displays on Wednesday. I can't tell you how special and important everyone at RN MARKET made me feel, to take all that time to help me succeed. The displays were beautiful and very professional looking.

During the seminar I had several attorneys comment on the exhibit. Several attorneys spent a good amount of time at my exhibit, they not only told me they would call but made sure to give me their cards also. One Attorney didn't have his cards with him, so he wrote his name on a piece of paper and handed it to me. I currently have 3 attorneys who send me several cases a month and another 15-20 who contact me several times a year.

It has almost been 12 months since I first contacted RN MARKET. Since then I have received 45 cases and have several attorneys who share my name with their colleagues.

Thank you RN MARKET for your LNC STAT program, your marketing package, and the attention that you spend with nurses to help them succeed!

UPDATE

It has been 5 years and I now have 20 attorneys, 10 that use me throughout the year consistently, and another 5 that use me periodically. I have stopped counting how many cases I have completed, but I have done hundreds of cases. With one attorney alone, I have received over 120 cases from his firm.

I have also been fortunate enough to be able to take on some pro bono cases. One of the cases involved a nurse that was fired that should not have been fired. It made me feel good to give back to a total stranger and be able to do it without having to worry about getting paid.

I have enjoyed the yearly Indulge conferences for the past three years and have never missed one. Besides taking the LNC STAT Advanced Certification Course, I have also taken the Certified Legal Nurse Investigator (CLNI) and the Certified Product Safety Specialist (CPSS) courses which have helped to increase my caseload and my income. I still speak to Veronica at least once a week and am even working on a case with her.

RN, ALNC, CLNI, CPSS - Ohio

I have recently finished Veronica's course and received my marketing package. My partner and I mailed out our first "mass mailing" of 52 packets to local attorneys about a month or so ago. We called prior to sending the packets out and we made follow up calls to all of the attorneys that received our packets. We just recently have taken lunch to one attorney who is interested in using us the next time he needs an Advanced Legal Nurse Consultant and we have a few more attorneys that want to meet with us within the next week. We are going to be mailing out a newsletter soon and more packets. We know it is going to just take time getting our name out there and a little bit of persistence. Our marketing materials look great and our Web site is very, very professional looking. I have no doubt we will soon be on our way to a very successful business!!!

Thank you Veronica!

Angela Rumbaugh
RN, ALNC - Iowa

I assume my story is like many others. I have two small children that have attended child care since only a few months old. With the exposure of frequent viral illnesses and continuous ear and sinus infections, we have been a "frequent flyer" to the doctor and urgent care centers. With my working full time, they often spent 10-11 hours in child care increasing their exposure.

In November, my daughter was nearly two years old when she acquired another illness and it ended in spending a week in the hospital with pneumonia. I vowed then that I needed to get her out of harms way. But I was not quick enough. In April, she spent another week in the hospital. In October, we had a near miss. With round the clock respiratory treatments and steroid/ antibiotic injections at the doctor's office, we were able to keep her home.

In November, I ordered my home study LNC STAT course and Advanced Legal Nurse Consultant Certification test. Working full time and having two small children, I was able get through the home study by February in time to attend the First Annual Indulge Conference. I was inspired by the energy and thrilled to be entering a field of true professionals.

I completed the class by taking the exam. That day I stayed after the exam and reviewed with other students different interviewing techniques. Up to that point I had been sending self created mailers without success. A few days later, I made a phone call to an attorney's office and asked for the person in charge of intake. As I was speaking to her, she was closed to everything I said. At that point, I said "isn't there a case that you are just not sure what to do with?" She paused and said "yes." So we discussed the basics and I agreed to review that record. Upon arrival to pick up the record, the attorney met me in the lobby. We had a short interview. He was extremely nice and less intimidating than I had envisioned. He basically stated that if all goes well, he had at least 50 cases that I could help him with. I had someone's voice ringing in my head and promptly said "bring it on" (with a smile). He also offered the names of several of "the best" attorneys in town and that I could use his name when contacting them.

I have yet to get all 50 cases, but I did leave my job. I have had other interviews and cases since that time. I certainly would not recommend to anyone to quit their job as quickly as I did. Marketing takes money and goes quickly when that primary income is missing. But I was happy when my 5 year old son's first day of kindergarten came and I could walk him to the door and kiss him good-bye. And believe it or not, my daughter (now 3 1/2 years old) has been healthier than ever with less time in child care. I would call that a success!

Wendy Duncan
RN, ALNC, CLNI - Florida

LNC STAT and Veronica changed my life this year! Back in the spring, I received a DVD in the mail from another Legal Nurse Consulting course. After watching it, I thought this sounds great! But the more that I researched the various course offerings the more I realized that this was going to cost a lot of money. I phoned or wrote emails to anyone that was listed for the courses. My questions were how long did it take to get their first job, and did they get any more afterwards? Everyone that I spoke with was very honest, and shared frustrations of not getting much work.

After a lot more online research, I found RN MARKET which was offering a course called LNC STAT. I phoned the office and left a message requesting to speak with someone. Later when my phone rang, I was shocked that not only was a representative from RN MARKET and LNC STAT returning my call, but the caller was none other than Veronica, the owner of RN MARKET herself!

Needless to say, I did order the LNC STAT Home Study course, and during the first few days in reviewing the course I received my first two cases! I was so excited that I phoned Veronica, and interrupted one of her LNC STAT classes with my enthusiasm! I completed those cases, and continue to obtain cases without much effort. The attorney calls that I get say that they got my name from an attorney whom I worked with previously. Having worked as an ICU/CCU and ER nurse for over 14 years, as well as having taught college, Advanced Legal Nurse Consulting provides me a different arena in which to provide my nursing knowledge. Right now, in some form or fashion I work almost daily to move my Advanced Legal Nurse Consulting business forward which includes working weekends. The remarkable thing is that I still have time for my family.

I still phone Veronica on a regular basis to let her know about my cases. She is the constant cheerleader always telling me to "go get 'em!"

Brian Howard
MSN, ARNP, FNP-C, ALNC - Kentucky

Wow! I don't know where to start. I took part of Veronica's LNC STAT course, the MARKET FOR SUCCESS 2 day workshop in February and I came home with a wealth of information. After the class, I sent out several packets and really didn't get any response with them even though I had made my pre-calls and post calls. I knew what the problem was. It was my lack of self-confidence. I still didn't know if I could write a report and really do this. It is not that I lacked the confidence in my nursing abilities and my knowledge in my field, but I didn't know how to write a report and I still had this gigantic fear of what to say to the attorney when I had him on the phone. I still get tongue tied.

I spoke several times to my brother who is head of sales where he works. He has the gift of gab and helped me practice several times with him. Then, I spoke again with Veronica and she helped to rid me of my fears. I took her Report Writing & Case Analysis 2 day workshop and I felt like I could really do this. I spoke up in the class and argued my point over the case that we were going over in class. I got my confidence.

I sent more packets out in June and didn't get much response from them. I then received a phone call from my friend Laura, who I met at Veronica's

Report Writing & Case Analysis workshop. She needed an expert witness on a case and wanted to know if I would be interested. Boy, I jumped on it! Her attorney contacted me and I worked up the case.

In the meantime, I received a call from an attorney that I mailed a packet to back in June. She contacted me in August and asked if I would be her ER expert witness. I gladly accepted. I have been in constant contact with her. I can't wait for the challenge. I know after having Veronica and her gang mentor me that I can really do this. I am now an official Legal Nurse Consultant! With Veronica as our leader, I am up for any challenge.

Thanks! Veronica

Regina L. Riggs
RN, BSN, CEN, CLNC - Kentucky

My objective in going to the Legal Nurse Investigator (CLNI) course offered by RN MARKET in Tampa was to prepare myself for work in the nursing field after many years of working in another profession. My clinical experience was in open heart surgery which gave me great satisfaction, but, because of the long hours standing scrubbed next to the surgeon, being on call every third night, more often than not being called in and the physically and emotionally draining tense atmosphere that accompanies open heart, I burned out and I really no longer had any interest in clinical nursing.

A varied and unusual career followed which included positions as an operating room supervisor in equine surgery and anesthesia at The Ohio State University, a member of the Motion Picture First Aid Union in Hollywood, an independent open heart nursing consultant, and a medical filmmaker for UCLA Medical Center.

I entered into and enjoyed a second vocation as a film cameraman, but, always kept my licenses current taking Legal Nursing oriented courses for continuing education. My interest in Legal Nursing led to me to pursue the Certified Legal Nurse Investigator (CLNI) course instructed by RN MARKET. To prepare for this course, I immediately ordered and completed the LNC STAT, Advanced Legal Nurse Consultant Certification Home Study course. I fondly recall my experience at RN MARKET as very informative and down to earth material was presented by professionals in their respective fields.

Legal Nurse Consulting 145

Since my CLNI certification, I have formed CLN Investigator 7, consulting with a private investigative firm, working with medical record tampering and insurance fraud. My experience with RN MARKET was time and money well invested. The education was absolutely invaluable.

Bill Sheehan
RN, ALNC, CLNI - New York

WOW! What an amazing 6-day course to advance our practice!!!!!! I believe that every Legal Nurse Consultant should take the LNC STAT Advanced Legal Nurse Consulting course and certification test who want to take their consulting business to the next level.

The LNC STAT course is extremely motivational and uplifting. Veronica, owner of RN MARKET, creates a relaxed setting with her magical personal touch, establishing a higher learning atmosphere. She is extremely knowledgeable in the fields of Legal Nurse Consulting, marketing and business, which is conveyed throughout her presentation of information and course materials. She takes difficult, confusing information especially for the new Legal Nurse Consultant and puts it into simple, easy-to-understand language.

Veronica is very proactive in helping Legal Nurse Consultants succeed and will go that extra step in assisting a nurse to obtain his/her professional edge and goals in getting cases. She also takes great pleasure in "pampering" her nurses with little surprises popping up during the week and always has lots of special chocolates at your fingertips.

One of the things about the course that appealed to me is that Veronica only allows a max of 6-10 people in each seminar to assure more individualized attention, questions, and learning opportunities from each other's expertise and experience. Veronica feels her teaching can be more effective with smaller groups in educating Legal Nurse Consultants in what it takes to get cases than with massive numbers of people crammed into a room.

This course definitely takes you to the next level, the advanced level of Legal Nurse Consulting.

After the week was completed, I felt as if I could conquer the legal world, obtaining a case from an attorney every time I walked into their office. I highly recommend a week with Veronica.

In addition, Veronica's marketing company, RN MARKET LLC, creates a very eminent image that illuminates through their logos, designs, paper qualities and Web sites, giving their Legal Nurse Consulting clients that professional "WOW Effect" edge.

Kristen Rapp
RN, BSN, ALNC, CLCP - California/Florida

Veronica,

I just wanted to let you know how much I enjoyed and learned from the LNC STAT home study program. It was like I was sitting in the classroom. The program was very professionally done. When I finished one disc, I couldn't wait to start the next one. The course was very complete, realistic, and easy to understand.

I also want to say that it is an inspiration just speaking with you on the telephone. I always feel empowered, energized, and like I can accomplish anything after I speak with you. You have truly found your niche in life.

Thanks for all of your help and expertise. I look forward to staying in touch with you and attending future conferences.

Nancy DiDonato
RN, CCM, MSCC, CNLCP, ALNC - Illinois

I have always needed extra money!! In addition to my fulltime position, I have worked many part time jobs; most have been routine floor nursing positions. I was tired of working for someone else, tired of the possibility of being stuck for more hours if the next shift didn't show up, tired of not eating properly, just plain tired of the floor nursing routine.

I wanted to be my OWN BOSS. I longed for something that would challenge my brain and make me look at nursing from a completely new and different point of view.

I read about Legal Nurse Consulting and it seemed to meet all of my needs. I investigated the program at a local law school. The cost was prohibitive ($10,000 without books & supplies). There was also the cost of commuting and the time needed to go to class. Some of the classes were offered in a sequence, and not offered each semester.

I decided that what I needed was a home study course where I could learn at my own pace. I went online and found several schools. One of the schools offering a home study program where the cost varied on the amount of mentoring one would need. Other schools online were just as expensive.

When I called these schools I never spoke to a nurse. I was usually transferred to a marketing person who could only answers questions that had prewritten answers.

And then one day, reading a nursing magazine, I found RN MARKET. I called and would you believe the OWNER, Veronica, called me back!! And what's more she is a nurse. She spent over an hour talking to me and was able to answer all of my questions and concerns. Her enthusiasm was so catching over the telephone, that I knew this was the program for me!

The price was within my budget, and there was no extra cost for mentoring!! There was even a case study in the packet. Additionally, each of the four DVD groups could be purchased separately.

The first three DVD's for the home study course are based on a live class presentation. I was able to learn so much more from the interactions of the students with the instructors. I did the case study on my own, and then compared it to the ones done by the students in the class. Veronica's honest input throughout the presentation gave me a true insider's view into the workings of an Advanced Legal Nurse Consultant. I found all the instructors on the DVD's to be very knowledgeable in each of their fields of expertise and they were able to answer questions posed to them.

The fourth DVD set and the companion MARKET FOR SUCCESS Workbook in and of themselves were worth every penny the program cost.

Veronica's enthusiasm for getting what you want out of life is mesmerizing. It's like getting a B-12 shot vicariously. Her presentation is simple and forthright. "Go out and get what you've worked for and earned. Learn from your mistakes. Stop making excuses for what you haven't done!" WHAT A FIND!!

UPDATE:

Based on our conversation a few weeks ago, I am sending you two pictures of the diamond and ruby earrings that I recently purchased as a "great going" gift to myself.

I took your home study Legal Nurse Consulting course last year, took the test and passed it. I started sending out my information packets everywhere this past January. In May I received two cases. I completed them within a month and was paid within 6 weeks. I made $6,900 on the two cases!!

Remembering what you said about rewarding yourself, I purchased the earrings and wear them with great pride. Thanks so much for your continued encouragement. I am now sending out more packets with follow up telephone calls.

I started my business in November. In May I received two plaintiff cases from a law firm. These two cases entailed a great deal of research, review and finally depositions. They were just recently settled in favor of the plaintiffs. That year I made $6900 just from these two cases. I then received another case from this law firm, as well as 9 other plaintiff cases. I earned over $30,000 on those cases. I advertised in several journals, however, everyone found me off my Internet Web site, made by RN Market.

What can one say, but THANK YOU, Veronica!!

Caryn A. Leifer
BA, RN, ALNC - New Jersey

Guess what? An attorney called me today. He is hired by an insurance company on nursing home cases. He said, "Well let me see, I have five charts on my desk," I nicely interrupted, "WELL GET THEM IN THE MAIL!". He laughed and said, "I like your energy". He is mailing the records on the first case early next week. He was very impressed with the Certified Legal Nurse Investigator credential. This is so much fun! Thanks for everything,

Laura Buttelwerth
RN, ALNC, CLNI, CPSS - Ohio

I thought you might be interested. I got my first client and am doing 3 cases for him. I gave him the first finished case and received this today from his paralegal (see below)! I'm very pleased! Thank you for the fine training!

Client Testimonial:
Caroline,

I thought you would be interested to know – the attorney was very pleased and impressed with your work product. He said you did an excellent job!

Everybody could use a positive to start the day!

Thanks, and I look forward to working with you in the future.

Paralegal

Caroline Nelson
RN, BSN, ALNC, CEN - Florida

My business partner and I had been doing basic chart organization, with accompanying timelines and summaries for about 7 years, and decided to make it a "real" business. In the course of our business development, we reached the decision that to achieve credibility we needed to take a Legal Nurse Consultant course. We attended the LNC STAT seminar in August in Las Vegas, Nevada. The information we gleaned from the seminar is so valuable. We came back raring to go, and actually had received a call for a case while we were in line at the airport. When we got home and started the case, we excitedly used the software that we purchased at the LNC STAT Seminar Smartdraw Legal Solution, and used tables from the Software CD Templates that came with the program, and we WOWed the attorney so much that he not only paid immediately, but has already contacted us for another case. We have become part of a Legal Nurse Consulting network that gives us tremendous support, and we are on our way to making this dream of a big business a reality.

Lissy Vogt
RN, MS, ALNC - Kentucky

Sandy Moss
RN, PAC, ALNC - Kentucky

In February, I took an online course about Legal Nurse Consulting, having an interest in Forensic Nursing and Legal Nursing. After the course, I had no idea how to proceed. I knew what a Legal Nurse Consultant did, but not how to proceed with that information. Then, I started looking into other courses. I knew I needed a live course to help with the "You go girl" factor!!! After a number of options, I took Veronica's course. She gave me the hands-on that I needed.

Towards the end of the course, Veronica subcontracted a real case to me, knowing I am an ER nurse, and that was what the client wanted. I did the case and got great feedback from Veronica. My first paycheck!!!!! I put my goals down on paper, which Veronica taught helps make them real, and come true. **My first year my goal is to make $10,000, and I'm there already!!**

With my Ultimate Marketing Package created by RN MARKET, I started getting names and sending out packets and making cold calls. While making a follow up call, I spoke with a paralegal to which I thought I had sent info to, but they never received it. After speaking with her, we made an appointment for me to meet the lawyer. At that meeting, he gave me my first 3 cases!

And I guess the rest is history. I still work fulltime and I also work continuously with this particular lawyer. He has kept me busy month after month!!! I get such great feedback from them! I get a great deal of satisfaction doing what I'm doing. I'm hoping within the next year I can quit altogether and do my Legal Nurse Consulting fulltime!!

I know I'm not working fulltime as a Legal Nurse Consultant yet, but that is one of my next goals! So, you know I will be doing it soon!

Caroline Nelson
RN, BSN, ALNC, CEN - Florida

Wanting to do something else with our nursing license Bev and I took an alternate Legal Nurse Consulting class last year in May. The course was very informative about what a Legal Nurse Consultant was and very pricey but after 4 months or so we still didn't have any cases. We had bills up the ying-yang and we were getting desperate. We just didn't know what we were doing wrong.

Then, we found RN MARKET LLC. We talked with Veronica and told her our story; we were very reluctant to order anything else since we spent so much money on the other Legal Nurse Consulting class, but Veronica explained her Ultimate Marketing Package to us. We ordered her marketing material and followed the guideline she outlined for us. We finally started getting responses, our marketing package looked very professional and the attorney's thought of us as professionals. We still needed more.

We saw that Veronica was offering a LNC STAT course and we needed it, but we needed it now, we just couldn't wait until January so we called Veronica. Veronica created a LNC STAT course just for us in our time of need. There are not any companies out there that I know of that not only cater to nurses but also to your personal needs. Thank you so much Veronica for making our dreams come true. The LNC STAT course helped us get more cases. When we took the course and became certified as Advanced Legal Nurse Consultants, it increased our caseload. This class gave us advanced knowledge needed to be successful.

I know it's hard to image that best friends can go into business together and be successful but I can't imagine it any other way. We currently are working actively on 2 medical malpractice cases and have 4 other cases on the back burner awaiting documentation.

One of our attorney's considers us his "secret in his back pocket," and he referred us to other attorneys that we have done cases for. In all since October of 2005, we have worked for 11 months and have had over 27 cases that we have worked on.

Veronica, thank you so much in believing in us. You treated us like we were your own sister. We love you!

UPDATE

After taking the LNC STAT Certification Course and the Certified Product Safety Course, 5 years later, we are in the 6 figure income and are doing several mass tort cases as well as regular reviews. This year alone we are anticipating doing more than 100,000 cases with several new contracts in the wind. Currently we have 59 independent nurse subcontractors and are anticipating hiring more.

Thank you so much Veronica in helping our business succeed!

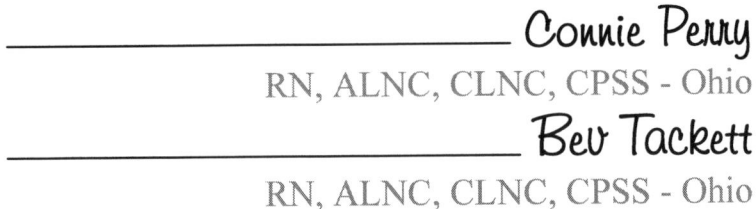

_____ Connie Perry
RN, ALNC, CLNC, CPSS - Ohio

_____ Bev Tackett
RN, ALNC, CLNC, CPSS - Ohio

I took the LNC STAT course in Las Vegas in August. It was a very intense week at which time I learned a great deal about how to write reports as well as how to market myself to attorneys. While there, I contacted a friend who was an attorney and asked him out to lunch when I returned home, under the auspices that I wanted to ask his advice regarding what my plans were to be a Legal Nurse Consultant.

When I cam home, I immediately began putting together my marketing packages.

I dressed appropriately, took him to lunch and began our conversation by asking questions about his practice and what he thought about utilizing Legal Nurse Consultants. He was more than happy to not only give me referrals, but to write letters to some of his fellow attorneys regarding my new business.

Within a week, I received copies of all of the letters he had written to about twenty attorneys. Out of the twenty attorneys, I got appointments with five of them.

I met with an attorney. He was very nice, asked me a lot of questions regarding my background. He even asked medical questions in regard to a case he was presently working on. He must have been impressed, because he took notes on some of my responses.

He finally told me he did have a small case he wanted me to look at and give my opinion on. I said I would be more than happy to do it.

I have completed that report. I also have appointments set up with two other attorneys.

What I have discovered in this business is that it is important not to get discouraged, to take the imitative, and to network. Always ask whatever attorney you are talking to if they know any other attorneys who might need your services.

The LNC STAT course has helped a great deal in giving me initiative and the ability to weed through reams of paperwork to find the needle in the haystack.

RN, BA, ALNC - Georgia

In 1998, I decided to seek a new avenue in my nursing career. After having invested ten years in the hospital clinical setting, I was tired and burned out from the hospital scene and was definitely ready for a change. Then, one day, I was looking through a nursing magazine and came across an advertisement on becoming a Legal Nurse Consultant. I decided to take the chance and borrowed the money to sustain me while I took the necessary courses, and the next thing I knew, I was on a plane to Atlanta to begin a 6-day seminar to become a Legal Nurse Consultant. By the end of the week, the "light bulb" had gone off, and I was very excited about my new career venture. I had always said when I was going to college for my first Bachelor of Science Degree in Sports Medicine that I would never go into nursing or law, the two professions at that time for which I had an immense dislike. Well, never say "Never!"

After I took the Legal Nurse 6-day course, I came home extremely motivated but was not quite sure how I was going to put all of my new knowledge together to begin my own business. The course I took was a beginner's course, but I felt that I needed to learn more in order to have the confidence that I required to go before an attorney. So, I continued to work in the hospital, putting off getting my business started. I had now fallen into the "dysfunctional comfort zone" at the hospital but had money coming into my pocket once again. During this time, I continued to keep up my Legal Nurse Certification by attending conferences and reading everything I could on the Legal Nurse industry. As time went on, working day in and day out in the hospital, and then my manager changing my shifts to nights, I was becoming more excited again about starting my own Legal Nurse Consulting business. It came down to working in the hospital for the next 20 years or becoming financially independent, working in my own Legal Nurse business.

When Veronica started her LNC STAT seminar, which included becoming an Advanced Legal Nurse Consultant, I was excited and passionate to have the opportunity to advance my profession and have the credentials after my name. I was becoming too advanced now for the beginning conferences, which were structured for the beginning Legal Nurse Consultant. I felt that the knowledge and professional tools that I acquired from the beginner courses and conferences were definitely valuable because they gave me my start; however, in order to really get myself out in the legal world, I needed a place to go where I could actually put the whole picture together, which I found through LNC STAT and my Advanced legal Nurse Consultant Certification.

I have reviewed numerous medical records and have developed exceptional analytical and investigative talents in evaluating records, identifying missing documents, tampering, and adherences to and deviations from Standards of Care, which I give to my experience as a nurse and Veronica's courses. After I took Veronica's LNC STAT course in April, my caseload has increased dramatically in just a few months. Since April, I have already completed close to 20 cases, and it seems that as each month goes by, my caseload keeps increasing towards finally making my vision of owning a successful business and being financially independent a reality.

Thank you, Veronica, for making this dream a reality!

Kristen Rapp
RN, BSN, ALNC, CLCP - California/Florida

"There's nothing like the real thing baby!" I have been trying to do my Legal Nurse Consulting business for the last 7 or 8 years. I attended seminars, went to school and bought tapes and books, all resulting in very limited or no success!!!.... Enter Veronica and RN Market. Studying real cases, sitting and critiquing with a real attorney. It was challenging, fun, rewarding, but mostly confidence building!!! I went to

Veronica's in Nov and Dec and already have MANY leads and two cases!

_____ *Sheryl Truman*
RN, ALNC, CLNI - Maine

I mailed out my first set of packets and did my follow-up calls today. I got three appointments over the next couple of days. First, let me tell you that all of the attorneys that I talked to knew my name from the materials. One attorney even commented on the fact that he usually throws away advertising but was so impressed with the content and professionalism of the package that he kept it. I eventually got him to set a meeting with me. Thanks everyone for a great job (again)!

_____ *Dianna Woodall*
RN, ALNC - Virginia

Thank you for getting back to me on all my questions. I had an interview today with an attorney and he is sending retainer and records for two cases with more to come. He certainly confirmed what you stated several times that there is a huge need and that I can be as busy as I want to be.

I cannot thank you and your staff enough. I am EXTREMELY excited yet equally nervous. He mentioned that attorneys are always asking each other if they know of any nurses they can use and that word of mouth will get me a long way.

Once again, a million thanks!!!! I will keep in touch.

Sandra Salomon
RN, BSN, MBA/HCM, ALNC – Arizona

Just returned last night from the Annual Florida Bar Convention, and it was great!! I would much rather do that for 3 days then walk into a lawyer's office cold. One of my giveaways was a total hit and I had people coming to the table to get them (and they had to take a packet of course!). Even some judges offered to pass along my information! Monday I plan to send follow up cards and make appointments with the 16 (16!!!) that are interested in meeting! Thanks for all your help with everything!

Julie Kovac
BS, RN, OCN, ALNC - Florida

I have been busy working in the home health field and working on a couple of my first cases on the side.

I just wanted to let you know that I really felt like I learned a lot from you when I was in Tampa for your class. It has helped me to be more forward and less shy in my approach with the attorney that I am working my second case for. The report writing was great for my confidence and so was the role play in explaining a case to an attorney. I recently did just that with my attorney and his paralegal. When I was finished and we had batted Q&A back and forth, he said I did a great job and gave me another case and paid his bill right then for the first one.

I am also working on a case that I agreed to be a testifying expert in. I agreed to it not long after I started sending out my marketing. It is now coming to fruition and it looks like it should be a money maker. The attorney had me review a huge pile of depositions and it may go to court. I am nervous and excited, but I really want to do this and do it well. I am going to review my CD on deposition that I purchased from you. I watched it once. It is excellent.

I really do appreciate the class and the meal that you provided us with when I was in Tampa. You are perfect at what you do. I will always think fondly of you both and what you taught me! Maybe I can get to another of your classes sometime.

Clare McBrayer
RN, CLNC - Kentucky

Veronica,

I had to take this time to tell you a story. I was a member of your LNC STAT program in August. I am so glad that I attended your ALNC certification program. I was and still am disabled from an accident three years ago. Although physically a struggle, I was able to complete your course. I am so excited to tell you about my first case. It was a very intensive project. This case paid for the entire cost of your program, and I still had enough left over to buy a set of earrings. All in 48 hours!

I can't express how much your program has done for me, it literally changed my life. Your books go with me everywhere. "The Legal Nurse Marketing Handbook and Report Writing and Case Analysis" are my bibles. Without them I never could have done a thorough and complete report on the case. In fact, my husband had to mail them to me overnight to Boston. The best part of this story is that I was hired for this case while I was in a Boston Hospital, all because my Web site caught their eye. I couldn't believe that I could be hired while recovering from multiple procedures. Due to continual adherence to all your programs, and books, I was able to present a professional, thorough, and substantiated report. The attorney was extremely pleased with the content and format of my work.

The entire RN Market package, and your one-on-one approach to learning, made it happen for me. I never hesitate to call your office and ask for help from your outstanding and patient staff. My Web site is amazing, and very personal to me, your staff did that for me. Now, I feel like I can take on whatever comes my way. The ALNC way.

Thank you Veronica, for your knowledge and support at all times. I have, and will continue to recommend LNC STAT to all my RN friends and acquaintances.

You and your LNC STAT program changed my life. I thank you and your professional staff for all you do. With best wishes to you all.

Mary Ellen Pakutinski
RN, FNP, ALNC - Florida

Dear Veronica, Thank you for the great conference. I felt empowered working with you and Ryan.

Rena Bowden
RN, CLNC, CPSS - Washington

Comfortable going out on the Street

Like you, within the walls of the hospital or clinic facility, I was very comfortable. We know how it all works and who to talk with and where to find what we need. Like you, I needed to do something different. Somewhere between the night shifts with all ten patients awake and August 31st 2005 at the New Orleans Airport/Katrina- turned into our receiving facility for thousands of sick, birthing and dying people. Seeing firsthand how the people of New Orleans lost all their choices forged my desire to choose what I wanted to do in life.

Veronica and Ryan at RN MARKET, teach, demonstrate and have you practice exactly what you need to know, how to get out of the facilities and onto the street. Then, when you are on the street, they are available to assist you. I have called Veronica from the West Coast to discuss case strategy, resulting in several direct referrals for my company. So, go learn from RN MARKET and then get out on the street, into the fresh air and sunshine. You guys ROCK!

Carmen Scherich
RN, ALNC - Washington

I am so glad I called you! After making several phone calls to attorneys, I felt like I was getting nowhere. I was leaving a lot of voice messages and having the secretaries take down my name and number. I even spoke to some attorneys that sounded interested...but no cases! I figured I would call you and tell you what I had been up to and see if you could give me some tips.

WELL, you told me to keep calling until I got a case, after making 2 more phone calls I got my first case! It took 2 minutes. The firm I called said they already had 2 legal nurse consultants on staff but she wanted my CV just in case they had an overflow. It was then that I told her that I also do Expert review in the OR and her voice lit up. We spoke about a case that she was working on and needed an expert. I am sending her my CV and the marketing package that I received from RN Market. I am sure she will be impressed (you and Matt did a great job).

I have an appointment on Monday with the attorney!

Shari Joiner
RN, ALNC - Michigan

I just wanted to let you know I just obtained my first case!!!!(actually the attorney is sending me 3!) I am so nervous!

Donna Lonschein
RN, ALNC - Massachusetts

When I was asked to write this up for Veronica I could not say no. I took LNC Stat. I worked for a friend doing LNC work and he always encouraged me to go out on my own. After looking at many of the courses offered out there I picked up the phone and called Veronica. Not only did she spend about three hours on the phone with me she gave me the confidence I needed to take the leap. I got my first case with an amazing attorney. She too had the confidence in me. I know that with the support of Veronica and her staff I can continue to strive to build my business. I am very excited of what the future holds for me in my business and I know it can only be a great success. Thanks Veronica & staff for all your continued support.

Ally Kayton
RN, MSN, NNP-BC, ALNC - Florida
www.kaytonlnc.com

CHAPTER 17
Conclusion

Do you think this is for you? What steps do you take next to secure the future of your nursing career? You now have an introduction to what life would be like as an Advanced Legal Nurse Consultant. It is up to you to decide what other tools, books or courses you will purchase to become a Legal Nurse Consultant. You will need to determine the cost and how you are going to finance your new venture. Taking a course that is very expensive does not mean that you are getting all the tools that you need to succeed. There are many nurses all across the country who take Legal Nurse Consulting courses ...but, the majority of these nurses are not even getting their first case. This is the reason RN MARKET LLC created the LNC STAT course. RN MARKET LLC designed the LNC STAT course to focus on the weak points where most Legal Nurse Consultants go wrong in their business. LNC STAT is set up so that you actually have all of the tools you need to get all the cases you want.

LNC STAT is the interactive and hands-on approach to getting cases as a Legal Nurse Consultant. Upon completion of the LNC STAT course and passing the test, you will be certified as an Advanced Legal Nurse Consultant (ALNC). The course is available as a live seminar or can be taken as a home study on DVD, iPod or online. You can also combine these options by splitting the days up. Why take two courses when all you need is one...LNC STAT by RN MARKET LLC. It is the most affordable and comprehensive Legal Nurse Consulting course around.

Why is LNC STAT different?

The unique feature about the LNC STAT program that singles it out from the rest is the devotion to the needs of nurses and Legal Nurse Consultants around the country. RN MARKET strives to take an interactive role in the education and success of nurses; not just to lecture them. You need to be able to market your business and secure the level of success you always wanted. All while having complete confidence in the program you choose.

Here are some things that set the LNC STAT course apart from the rest of the courses that are out there:

- ✓ Each seminar is limited to 6-10 people for a more interactive and hands-on experience.

- ✓ The seminars are often held in luxurious hotel suites to create a more private and comfortable atmosphere.

- ✓ You get to do a case from start to finish the way that you would get a case from an attorney (you can keep it as a sample case).

- ✓ Full textbooks are included instead of books in outline format so you can reference them at any time you need.

- ✓ You walk away with the tools that will help you later on when you are doing your own cases such as letters, forms, agreements, contracts, invoices, and fee schedules in a template format so you can use them over and over again.

- ✓ This software, 2010 edition, contains 26 different letters, forms, agreements, contracts, invoices and fee schedules.

✓ You walk away with the tools that will help you later on when you are creating your cases including another software in template format so that you can make your reports.

✓ This software contains 12 different templates that you will use over and over again to create your reports including a screening form, intake form, invoice, demand letter, outline, timeline, chronology, fee schedule, contract, invoice, fax page, and calendar.

✓ Your questions are answered during and after the seminar.

✓ You will be able to join RN MARKET's private forum online for free where you can ask questions, talk to other Advanced Legal Nurse Consultants and exchange cases.

✓ You will be able to have the Ultimate Marketing Tool Kit, a marketing package that has been proven to make you successful. The number one selling and most effective marketing package for nurses in the country. RN MARKET is the first and only company that offers full-service marketing and mentoring to nurses.

178......

APPENDIX A
Continuing Education, Test, and Certificate Information

This book can be used as an introduction course to get you started as a Legal Nurse Consultant. After reading this book you can email RN MARKET at info@rnmarket.com to get information about the online certificate exam. After paying the fee and passing the online exam, you will be awarded 8 CE units and the Introduction to Legal Nurse Consulting Certificate will be available to you immediately after taking the online exam. This says that you have passed the Introduction to Legal Nurse Consulting course. With these skills you can start your Legal Nurse Consulting practice. But remember, there is still a lot you have to learn to get real success in this field. To get real success as a Legal Nurse Consultant we suggest getting advanced training by taking the LNC STAT course. There you can earn the Advanced Legal Nurse Consultant (ALNC) credential. The LNC

STAT course will give you all the tools you will need to become successful as a Legal Nurse Consultant.

APPENDIX B
RN MARKET Accreditation Information

RN MARKET is an approved educational provider of continuing education for nurses for the Florida Board of Nursing and for the District of Columbia Board of Nursing (Washington D.C).

Upon completion of the course and exam offered through this book you will be provided with 8 CE units from RN MARKET LLC approved of by the State of Florida Board of Nursing and the District of Columbia Board of Nursing (Washington D.C).

Upon completion of the LNC STAT Course, you will be provided with 50.4 CE units from RN MARKET LLC approved of by the State of Florida and the District of Columbia Board of Nursing (Washington D.C.).

Upon completion of the Certified Legal Nurse Investigator Course, you will be provided with 33.6 CE units from RN MARKET LLC approved of by the State of Florida and the District of Columbia Board of Nursing (Washington D.C.).

Upon completion of the Certified Product Safety Specialist Course, you will be provided with 25.2 CE units from RN MARKET LLC approved of by the State of Florida and the District of Columbia Board of Nursing (Washington D.C.).

Upon completion of the 2-Day Success Internship, you will be provided with 12 CE units from RN MARKET LLC approved of by the State of Florida and the District of Columbia Board of Nursing (Washington D.C.).

Upon completion of Case Strategies for the 21st Century, you will be provided with 16.8 CE units from RN MARKET LLC approved of by the State of Florida and the District of Columbia Board of Nursing (Washington D.C.).

Upon completion of The Forensic Workshop, you will be provided with 25.2 CE units from RN MARKET LLC approved of by the State of Florida and the District of Columbia Board of Nursing (Washington D.C.).

In order to receive the credits, please submit via email to info@rnmarket.com your nursing license and complete name with the address you would like your certificate mailed to. If you are a nurse from the State of Florida, your continuing education hours will be submitted directly to your board. If you are from another state or country, the certificate to submit your continuing education to your state will be provided. Please check with your state to ensure that your credits will be approved.

For individual LNC STAT workshop CEs, submit as previously described and see below:

- Legal Nurse Essentials Workshop - 8.4 CE
- Report Writing & Case Analysis Workshop - 16.8 CE
- Contracts & Fee Schedules Workshop - 8.4
- Market for Success Workshop - 16.8 CE

See RN MARKET's selection of approved courses online at www.CEBroker.com. CE Broker can track your CEs for you if you are in the State of Florida or District of Columbia (Washington D.C.). RN MARKET's continuing education credits are accepted in all 50 states for nursing CEUs.

The Introduction to Legal Nurse Consulting Certificate is granted to those who successfully completed the course offered in this book and the exam administered by RN MARKET, LLC.

The ALNC, CLNI, CPSS and FCEA credentials are exclusive certification marks of the LNI Institute, Inc. The credentials are granted to those who successfully complete the LNC STAT (ALNC), Certified Legal Nurse Investigator (CLNI), Certified Product Safety Specialist (CPSS) or Certified Forensic Criminal Evidence Analyst (FCEA) course including homework, case, and certification exam administered by RN MARKET LLC. Upon completion of the course you choose to take, with a passing grade, you will be certified for two years and will be able to use the credential that you have received. After the two years, you may maintain your certification by submitting 15 hours of approved medical-legal instruction every year.

Call RN MARKET for details and for approval of medical-legal instruction accepted by the LNI Institute, Inc. Check the LNC STAT, CLNI, CPSS, FCEA and EMLS schedules for seminar or workshop locations or dates or for information on home study courses.

There are no other licenses or certifications needed to practice as an Advanced Legal Nurse Consultant other than the ALNC credential. RN MARKET is the only official approved educational provider for LNI Institute, Inc. RN MARKET is the only education company approved of to teach the courses and certifications discussed in this book.

Association

The International and American Association of the Legal Nurse Industry (IAALNI) can provide education and promotes the advancement of nurses in any Legal Nurse area of practice. For more information or to join the association, go to www.IAALNI.org.

186……

APPENDIX C
Standards of Practice

Mission

The primary mission of the ALNC, CPSS, CLNI, FCEA or EMLS is to provide high quality services to organizations in need of medical records review, interpretation, or analysis that meet the standards enforced by the LNI Institute, Inc. An ALNC, CPSS, CLNI, FCEA or EMLS offer services for plaintiff as well as defense clients and can locate and/or act as testifying experts. The defining feature of the ALNC, CPSS, CLNI, FCEA or EMLS is the rigorous hands-on training achieved while meeting the live case training requirements. In addition to passing the certification exam, each student is required to complete all homework, casework and presentations and meet the standards set forth by the LNI Institute, Inc in this Standards of Practice Declaration.

Purpose of the LNI Standards of Practice

Professional ethics and quality of work are at the core of the ALNC, CPSS, CLINI, FCEA, or EMLS Certifications. The Certification Holder has an obligation to adhere to basic values, ethical principles, and ethical standards set forth by LNI Institute, Inc. The LNI Institute Standards of Practice sets forth these values, principles, and standards to guide Certification Holders' conduct and quality of work. This Standards of Practice Declaration is relevant to all Certification Holders and students, regardless of their professional functions, the settings in which they work, or the clients to which they provide services.

Standards of Practice Principles

Certification Holders must meet or exceed the requirements listed herein in order for their certification to be valid.

1) *The Role of the Advanced Legal Nurse Consultant or Expert of Medical Legal Specialties When Working on a Case*
   a) Assist with obtaining medical records
   b) Identify, interpret and review medical records for merit
   c) Identify missing records
   d) Screen medical records for tampering
   e) Review hospital policies and procedures

f) Define adherence to and deviations from the applicable Standards of Care
g) Consult with health care providers
h) Develop brief or comprehensive written reports
i) Conduct medical and nursing literature searches
j) Analyze and compare expert witness reports
k) Attend depositions, trials, review panels, arbitrations, and mediation hearings
l) Interview plaintiff and defense clients, witnesses and experts
m) Identify factors that caused or contributed to the alleged damages/injuries
n) Identify and locate expert witnesses
o) Assist in exhibit preparations
p) Prepare interrogatories
q) Prepare a chronology of events or timeline for the case

2) *Behavior*

The Certification Holder must act in a professional manner at all times and refrain from abusive and/or inappropriate language towards any client or colleague in their field of practice.

The Certification Holder must act in a manner representative of their profession, training, education and certification while understanding that any acts, positive or negative, reflect not only on themselves but on those other professionals practicing in the same field of practice.

3) *Responsibilities to the Client*
Certification Holder must retain all non-public information obtained from Client as confidential and agrees not to release or disseminate, in any fashion nor via any medium, any such information unless Consultant has obtained prior written authorization of Client.

The Certification Holder must provide work in a manner which is consistent with skills and techniques taught in the corresponding Certification curriculum and must meet the quality standards of the client.

The Certification Holder must adhere to any contracts or agreements arranged between themselves and any client or associate related to their field of practice.

4) *Responsibilities to Colleagues*
The Certification Holder must treat other colleagues with the same respect, fairness and courtesy that they would expect from any other

colleague.

The Certification Holder must adhere to any contracts, agreements, and/or fees arranged between themselves and any subcontracting professionals or consultants providing cases for subcontracting.

5) *Certification Requirements*
The Certification holder must clearly inform their clients and/or subcontractors of the governing body for their certification, LNI Institute, Inc., either verbally or in writing.

6) *Certification Holder Complaints*
A complaint may be submitted by any client or colleague for any breach of the LNI Institute Standards of Practice.

Each complaint will be investigated by the LNI Institute President or by an official appointed by the President.

The Certification Holder may receive no more than three complaints from clients or colleagues. If three complaints are received, the Holder's Certification(s) will be revoked.

Upon revocation of the certification, the holder

must remove any information related to the certification from their documentation and is required to cease and desist from using their certification(s) in their practice.

If a Certification Holder has more than one Certification from LNI Institute and three valid complaints have been received, all Certifications governed by this Standards of Practice Declaration may be revoked.

Any colleague to a Certification Holder is under the obligation to report any breaches or complaints if they are certified under this Standards of Practice Declaration.

Complaints must be formally submitted to LNI Institute, Inc in writing and send via mail, fax or email.

By using the ALNC, CLNI, CPSS, FCEA or EMLS credential and certification you agree to the policies and standards discussed herein.

Bibliography

[1] Institute of Medicine. 2000. To Err Is Human: Building a Safer Health System. L. T. Kohn, J. M. Corrigan, and M. S. Donaldson, eds. Washington, D.C: National Academy Press.

[2] Bond CA, Raehl CL, Franke T. Clinical pharmacy services, hospital pharmacy staffing, and medication errors in United States hospitals. Pharmacotherapy. 2002 Feb;22(2):134-47.

[3] Ferguson II, Theodore K. Applied investigative techniques for medical investigations. Zoey publishing. 2006 Jan:17-30.

References

Castellana, Veronica, and Sanchez, Ryan, *The Legal Nurse Marketing Handbook, Fourth Edition,* Zoey Publishing, Tampa, Florida, 2009.

Castellana, Veronica, and Sanchez, Ryan, *Market for Success, Second Edition – Second Printing,* Zoey Publishing, Tampa, Florida, 2006.

Castellana, Veronica, and Sanchez, Ryan *Legal Nurse Essentials,* Zoey Publishing, Tampa, Florida, 2009.

Castellana, Veronica, and Sanchez, Ryan *Report Writing & Case Analysis,* Zoey Publishing, Tampa, Florida, 2009.

Hoback, Sherry, Rhonda Ladner, and Castellana, Veronica, *Report Writing & Case Analysis; Case Kit,* Zoey Publishing, Tampa, Florida, 2006.

Castellana, Veronica, and Sanchez, Ryan *Contracts & Fee Schedules,* Zoey Publishing, Tampa, Florida, 2009.

Ferguson, Theodore K., *Applied Investigative Techniques for Medical Investigations,* Zoey Publishing, Tampa, Florida, 2006.

Web Site References

RN Market, LLC
www.RNMARKET.com

LNC STAT - Advanced Legal Nurse Consultant (ALNC) and Expert of Medical Legal Specialties (EMLS)
www.LNCSTAT.com

LNI Institute, Inc.
www.LNIInstitute.com

International & American Association of the Legal Nurse Industry
www.IAALNI.org

Certified Product Safety Specialist (CPSS)
www.ProductSafetySpecialist.com

Certified Forensic Criminal Evidence Analyst (FCEA)
www.TheForensicWorkshop.com

Legal Nurse Courses
www.LegalNurseCourses.com

196......